INDIAN
FIGHTER

THE STORY OF NELSON A. MILES

INDIAN
FIGHTER

BY RALPH EDGAR BAILEY

Maps by James MacDonald
Frontispiece by Leslie Goldstein

William Morrow and Company   New York 1965

Grateful recognition is given to
Stephen E. Ambrose
of Johns Hopkins University,
for reading and criticizing
the manuscript.

1321667

TO RODNEY

Maps

CONTENTS

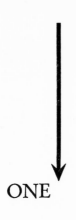

ONE

THE EARLY YEARS— CIVIL WAR

THE tall young officer bent low over the neck of his black charger and gently urged him to even greater speed. Minié balls splattered around horse and man in a hail of metal that threatened to cut them down as they raced along the immediate rear of the Union Army line.

Exploding shells burst into angry plumes of death and churned the ground into geysers of flying dirt. So terrific was the boom of Confederate field artillery and the rattle of Rebel small-arms fire that it seemed no horse could have heard what his master said; but the mettlesome black appeared to understand what this big blond stripling with the ice-blue eyes and the quiet voice expected of him.

9

Lieutenant Nelson Appleton Miles, aide-de-camp to Brigadier General Oliver Otis Howard, was hastening back from an observation post on high ground to report on the movement of enemy troops in the Battle of Fair Oaks in Virginia on June 1, 1862. His report might save the Union Army from defeat. Every second counted in getting his information to General Howard.

As Miles glanced up at the charging Union line, he saw the mounted colonel of a key regiment drop his waving sword, turn in the saddle, and topple to the ground. Within seconds the charging blue line started to waver. Men broke ranks and began to run toward the rear. With their leader dead they had no heart to stand up under the withering enemy fire.

Miles slowed his mount to a trot. As a staff officer he knew that it was vital for this particular regiment to hold its key position. He had intended to advise General Howard that the regiment be reinforced at once. But if this fighting unit fled in disorder now, the Confederates would pour through and the Union flank would be exposed. The enemy might roll up the whole Army before reinforcements could be sent in. Of what use would his report be then?

A minié ball plowed through the crown of his wide-brimmed black hat. His horse whickered in pain as another metal pellet grazed its rump. He had difficulty in controlling the animal. Miles sized up the situation on the battlefield almost instantly. These panic-stricken men must be stopped—at once! He reined in his horse, turned him around, and spurred back toward the disorderly mass of fleeing men.

Some of the blue-clad soldiers were already throwing down their weapons and stripping off their knapsacks and blanket rolls so that they could run faster. Desperately their officers were trying to rally them, but with no success. Panic had seized the men, and it was plain that they were wholly intent upon getting out of range of the murderous Confederate fire as quickly as they could. They needed the example of one courageous man to stiffen their morale.

Nelson Miles's galloping horse reached the retreating regiment. Miles waved his wide-brimmed, gold-corded black hat in the air and shouted, "Boys, follow me!" He waved his black hat again, indicating that the men were to turn around and charge the enemy.

"Fix bayonets!"

A few men set up a cheer. The young officer was ready to lead them into that hail of enemy lead. Could they do less than follow? They fixed bayonets and faced about. Others quickly followed; junior officers and sergeants were reforming the companies and platoons.

"Charge bayonets!"

The black hat waved the men onward. There were more cheers now, and the blue line held steady. Soon Nelson Miles was able to lead a countercharge.

He was in the thick of it. Minié balls tore through his hat and uniform, splattered the ground all around him, cut down some men in the charging blue line. Suddenly

Miles felt a minié ball sting one arm. Another lamed his horse. But the cheering men in blue were following him with a will, their courage almost as high as their spirit had been low only a few minutes before. They yelled defiance as they countercharged the Rebel line. The enemy had taken the first shock of the unexpected move, then had begun to fall back under its impact.

Miles knew he was losing a considerable amount of blood, but he managed to cling to the saddle despite increasing weakness. There was no time to attend to the wound. His horse stumbled and whickered in pain, but Miles could spare it no attention.

The Union countercharge began to slow down as the reformed Rebel line held. Miles hoped desperately that he could keep to the saddle. He must not fall until reinforcements could come up. Surely, by now, General Howard must know they were needed.

The courage and spirits of the men had returned, and the blue line was firmer. Because he forced himself to sit erect in the saddle the men had no suspicion that Nelson Miles had been wounded. The frantic antics of his painfully wounded horse could have been the result of battle excitement.

"Just a little longer, men! Help is on the way!" Miles encouraged the men when he saw some of them again begin to waver, although all he had to back his promise was a fervent prayer. "Hold on!"

Again the black hat waved in a wide arc. Miles forced himself to sit even straighter, as though he were escaping the hail of lead unharmed. It seemed that he could not keep to the saddle a moment longer or control his increasingly crazed horse, when he heard a wave of cheering behind him. He glanced around and saw another regiment, bayonets fixed, come charging into the fray. Reinforcements had arrived in time!

Still cheering their unknown leader, the badly shattered regiment fell back in order through the reinforcing regiment and marched to the rear. Now Miles and his wounded horse made their way as fast as they could to General Howard's headquarters. There he found that Howard himself had been wounded. But the Union forces at last were in undisputed control of the battlefield of Fair Oaks. The Confederate attempt to raise the siege of Richmond had failed. Nelson Miles's quick thinking and courageous action had saved the day for the Union Army.

Miles felt no particular sense of elation, however. He believed that he had only done his duty. He had happened to be the man on the spot when a new leader was needed, and he had acted instinctively. The fact that a lieutenant —and not a regularly assigned line officer at that—had taken over command of a retreating and badly disorganized regiment at a critical moment in battle seemed to him natural enough.

Nearly every day of his earlier life had contributed in some degree to his training for that battle. He was born in 1839 in Westminster, Massachusetts, where his family owned a small farm and lumber mill. Ever since he could remember, Nelson Miles had wanted to be a soldier. He had lived the life of a soldier in his favorite childhood games. Long before he could ride himself, he had sat in front of his father and held the reins of his horse. By the time he was eight, he was taking every hurdle—stone wall, fence, and fallen tree—in the countryside on his own horse, much to the dismay of his mother and his older sisters and brother. Hunting, trapping, fishing, wrestling, and skating occupied more of his time and thought than schoolwork.

When he was sixteen, Nelson Miles agreed to go to Boston as an apprentice clerk to John Collamore in a crockery shop. Only because he was an obedient son, who respected his father as much as he loved him, did young Miles agree to go into business and give up his long-cherished hope of trying for an appointment to West Point. But all the while he longed for a military career. He could not forget that there had been a Miles in every war the United States had fought, and the adventure of Indian fighting on the western frontier, now rapidly opening up to settlement, gripped his imagination.

By the time the Civil War broke out, Miles had served five years with Collamore and had begun to help run the business. Perhaps his father had been right after all; perhaps he could go as high as he wanted to in business. At first his insufficient schooling was a severe handicap, but he tried to make up for his lack of education by attending evening lectures and classes, studying until far into the night on a wide range of subjects.

Military strategy and tactics interested him most. He

had begun to study the masters of the arts of war—Alexander, Napoleon, Washington—even before moving to Boston. As the inevitable outbreak of war neared, he took lessons from a French army colonel who conducted a class for young men in Boston and drilled nightly in Dorchester, where he lived. By the time of the Battle of Fair Oaks he believed he already knew more military theory than most officers anywhere near his age.

At the beginning of the war, he spent $2500 from his savings and borrowed more money to raise and equip Company E, 22d Massachusetts Regiment of Volunteers, an infantry regiment. The men of Company E elected him captain by acclamation, so much confidence did they have in him as a leader. But the governor of Massachusetts gave the commission as captain to an older man for political reasons, and Miles found himself marching off to war in Colonel Henry Wilson's volunteers as first lieutenant in the very company he had spent his own money to equip!

He had not volunteered for the honor of leading Company E, however, but rather to help defend his country and to preserve the Union. If he must yield first place in Company E, for the present, that was all right with him. His day would come; he had no doubt of it. But he made no bones about his contempt for men with little military preparation or ability who were appointed to command troops. He made a lifelong enemy of the governor of Massachusetts by his open criticism of the shabby way he believed he had been treated. The enmity would come back to injure him later. All his life Miles fearlessly, if tactlessly, criticized men whom he felt to be inferior in ability when they stood in the way of getting a job done quickly and well.

Miles settled down to routine company work. Soon he was carrying most of the load and, during the first year of the war, enjoying it. But always he was trying to find ways to get things done better and faster. And always he continued studying military strategy and tactics.

Word gets around—especially in the Army.

It came as no surprise, but as a great satisfaction, when General Howard sent for him and asked him to join his staff as aide-de-camp. General Howard was a heavily bearded Maine man, a West Pointer, so it was an even greater honor for a professionally untrained volunteer to be asked to join his staff. Howard, less than ten years older than Miles, had won his spurs at the First Battle of Bull Run, one of the few officers on either side who deserved credit in that battle. Miles got along well with him from the first. While serving as aide to General Howard, he realized again how valuable his business training had been.

General Howard had no more trusted aide than Nelson Miles by the time the Army of the Potomac had fought to within seven miles of Richmond, intent upon capturing the Confederate capital. On May 31, 1862, at a place called Seven Pines, the Rebel General Joseph E. Johnston had attacked the Federal troops under General George B. McClellan. The action was indecisive.

The next day the battle had been resumed at Fair Oaks. It was there that Howard had sent Miles forward to keep

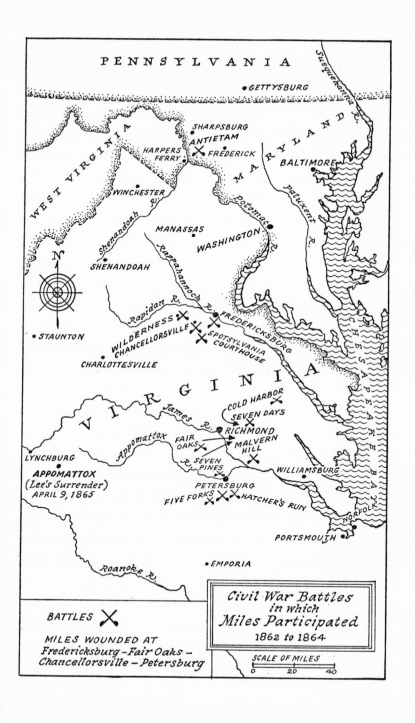

PENNSYLVANIA

• GETTYSBURG

Susquehanna R.

WEST VIRGINIA

SHARPSBURG
ANTIETAM ✕ FREDERICK
HARPERS FERRY

MARYLAND

BALTIMORE •

WINCHESTER

Potomac R.

Patuxent R.

Shenandoah R.

MANASSAS

WASHINGTON •

N

SHENANDOAH •

Rappahannock R.

• STAUNTON

Rapidan R.

WILDERNESS ✕ ✕ FREDERICKSBURG
CHANCELLORSVILLE ✕
SPOTSYLVANIA COURTHOUSE

• CHARLOTTESVILLE

VIRGINIA

COLD HARBOR ✕
SEVEN DAYS

James R.

FAIR OAKS ✕ • RICHMOND
MALVERN HILL ✕

LYNCHBURG

Appomattox R.

SEVEN PINES

WILLIAMSBURG •

CHESAPEAKE BAY

APPOMATTOX
(Lee's Surrender)
APRIL 9, 1865

PETERSBURG
FIVE FORKS ✕ ✕ HATCHER'S RUN

NORFOLK

PORTSMOUTH •

Roanoke R.

• EMPORIA

BATTLES ✕

MILES WOUNDED AT
Fredericksburg–Fair Oaks–
Chancellorsville–Petersburg

Civil War Battles
in which
Miles Participated
1862 to 1864

SCALE OF MILES
0   20   40

an eye on the enemy and, as it turned out, to get his first taste of command in battle.

With General Howard out of action, Miles was transferred to the staff of popular white-bearded Major General Edwin V. Sumner, commanding the Second Corps. Because of his deep voice, Sumner was known among officers and men alike as "Bull." Miles quickly took to the gruff-voiced general and to his job as adjutant. Sumner came to have much confidence in his new adjutant's judgment within a short time. Already he knew of Miles's calm courage.

After Fair Oaks there began one of the hardest-fought campaigns of the Civil War. The North struggled to take Richmond and the South just as stubbornly fought to hold the capital of the Confederacy.

McClellan opened what was to have been the North's decisive drive on Richmond on June 27. He was a fine soldier and an excellent organizer, but he lacked that determined drive that gets things done on the battlefield.

Before the Seven Days' Battle even began, McClellan's communications were cut. A daring ride by Confederate General J. E. B. Stuart's cavalry around the Union Army was unknown to McClellan until too late. He had no inkling of what had happened until his forces were committed to battle.

Soon the Union Army met intense fire from one flank as General Thomas "Stonewall" Jackson attacked in strength. McClellan was in danger of encirclement, or at least of having his flank driven in. His whole line might be rolled up.

McClellan had to know quickly what was going on behind the Rebel lines!

Behind the Union position there stood a tall pine tree. If a man could climb that tree and stay alive long enough, he might get the information McClellan so desperately needed. The Union commander could then determine whether he should try to hold his present line or retreat to save his Army.

Sumner glanced at the tree. "If we only had a man who could, and dared, climb that tree," Sumner shouted loud enough for his young adjutant to hear above the din, "we could get McClellan the information he needs. But I won't order any man up there. It's almost certain suicide."

Nelson Miles stepped forward and saluted. "Sir, I can climb that tree if a few iron spikes are driven into the trunk."

General Sumner nodded. "Yes, I think you could, Miles," he said, for he vividly remembered the incident at Fair Oaks. Perhaps he had hoped Nelson Miles would accept this challenge, too.

Within minutes the headquarters train armorer sent the spikes, along with a soldier who knew how to drive the spikes so that they would support a man's weight. The man rapidly hammered them in.

Then, spike by spike, Miles climbed until he stood at the very top. He was within range of enemy sharpshooters, and of enemy cannon as well, if they cared to waste ammunition on him. Confederate minié balls whizzed past him in such numbers that he scarcely noticed them. They sounded like a swarm of angry yellow jackets. The tree trunk, he quickly discovered, was much too small to serve as a shield for his body. For all practical purposes he was completely exposed to enemy fire, a wonderful target for every sharpshooter within range.

The Confederates had left a few men in their extensive earthworks. These soldiers kept up a steady fire at the Union troops, but Miles could see that there were wide gaps in the Rebel lines. The enemy's regimental bands had also been left behind. They were playing such stirring tunes as "Dixie" and "Bonnie Blue Flag" to deceive the Union Army into believing that the enemy force was still safe behind its entrenchments. McClellan was supposed to think the Rebels were set for a frontal attack. Instead, Miles saw that Rebel troops were massing on the banks of the Chickahominy River for another assault on the Union lines. It was a carefully prepared trap for McClellan.

Miles prayed that he might be spared long enough to get down from the tree and report to General Sumner. McClellan must receive a warning in time to act.

Now the enemy fire increased. It seemed that every sharpshooter in the Rebel lines was aiming at him. Minié balls cut through his hat. They tore at his uniform, and one was deflected off his belt buckle. He tried to shield himself as much as he could as he backed down the line of spikes, a step at a time, but every second seemed that it might be his last. He thought of shouting down his information, but he knew he could not be heard above such a din of firing.

He felt that an eternity passed before his feet touched

the ground. He found General Sumner and his staff anxiously awaiting his report. He told what he had seen, and one of Sumner's aides quickly spurred off to McClellan with the vital information.

"Well done, Miles!" boomed Sumner. "Well done!"

Miles felt as much rewarded as though he had received a medal. He didn't know until long afterward that General Sumner had told Howard, "That young man will be promoted or get himself killed." Indeed, Sumner had not forgotten Fair Oaks and the lost regiment. Nor would the general forget Miles's brave act that day.

Then came the Seven Days' battle of the Peninsula campaign, a series of sharp, fierce engagements.

During the fast-moving battle, General Sumner told Miles that two Union batteries had been cut off beyond a forest. General Lee had moved too swiftly for them to retreat.

Miles had wondered about the posts. Two batteries of field artillery, men, guns, caissons, ammunition, and horses were too much to sacrifice to the enemy if there was any hope of saving them. He thought he had a solution to the general's problem and asked permission to make a suggestion.

With a small detachment of Pioneers, he proposed to cut a narrow road through the forest. On it reinforcements could reach the guns and drive the enemy off long enough for the batteries to escape. The dense woods would cover the men cutting the road, he pointed out, and the Rebels would not suspect what was happening until too late.

The general looked doubtful. He didn't want to sacrifice more men, and it was likely that Confederate artillery fire would pour into the woods if the opposing forces had any inkling of the maneuver being attempted. Wouldn't the ring of the axes give away the plot, he asked? The deafening rattle of heavy firing all around them answered his question.

Sumner nodded decisively. Miles had his permission to go ahead!

Quickly he rounded up a detachment of Pioneers, specially trained, work-hardened soldiers whose job was to build and repair roads and bridges for the Army. Clearing a path through the dense forest at top speed proved to be a severe test of endurance, however. The men willingly expended every ounce of their energy, but a few could not keep up the pace. When one man slumped forward, Miles took the exhausted soldier's axe himself. Many of the other Pioneers saw him fell a tree quickly and expertly before handing the axe back to its owner. As the men chopped, there was a low buzz of conversation from man to man. Nelson Miles was respected by the officers and men of the entire corps after his heroic charge at the head of the leaderless regiment at Fair Oaks. But now there was real affection for him among the men of the Pioneer unit. It wasn't often that an officer pitched in to help his men. He had lost no shred of discipline in becoming one of them for a moment.

Hour by hour trees were felled, their boughs chopped off, and the logs dragged to one side of the rude path. It seemed to Miles that the minutes dragged. He could hear the heavy rattle of small-arms fire and the occasional boom of a field piece on the other side of the woods. He suspected that the Rebels were already attacking the two encircled Union batteries.

There was no time to cut a road wide enough for the endangered guns. Even more time would be wasted pulling out the tree stumps, which would block the wheels of the guns and caissons and injure the horses unless they were removed. But even on the narrow road they were building in such a hurry, infantry reinforcements could be rushed to the front. The fresh troops would take the Rebels by surprise. The two batteries might be able to escape by another road.

Coffee and food were brought up to the men from field kitchens and Miles allowed them brief rest periods. When a man was too exhausted to go on, a fresh Pioneer was sent in to replace him, but for Nelson Miles there was no rest and little time for food. Even with his great physical strength he was bone tired.

Now and then he would order spikes driven into the trunk of a tall tree, and he would climb it to determine how much farther his men had to cut before the two batteries could be reached. All the while small-arms fire and the occasional boom of a field piece did indeed drown out the ring of the axes.

At last Miles climbed a particularly high tree. Now he could see the besieged batterymen firing their field pieces. The smoke was heavy from cannon and small-arms fire.

He noticed a movement off to one side of the Rebel line and suspected that the gray-coated infantrymen were forming for a bayonet charge on the guns. The artillerymen would stand no chance against such a charge once the Rebels were among the cannon; they would be heavily outnumbered. Time was short if the field pieces were to be saved.

Miles backed down the line of spikes and summoned one of the Pioneers to carry the message to General Sumner. The begrimed soldier saluted and sprinted back through the forest path.

Within minutes soldiers were padding swiftly through the ready-made forest path, guns at the ready, bayonets fixed. They jumped over logs and dodged stumps. The firing and yelling ahead were increasing to a deafening roar.

Miles only hoped his job had been done in time.

The Union reserves deployed through the woods and burst upon the attackers from flank and center. Their fire, Miles could see as he climbed the observation post again, had driven back the Rebel charge against the guns. The Union battery commanders quickly hitched their horses to gun limbers and caissons and dashed off furiously down a side road that would take them around the woods and back into their own lines.

Time and again the Rebels charged the rescuing Union infantry, determined to win something for their great effort. But now the firepower of the Union troops was so heavy that the enemy was driven back. Then the rescuing troops themselves retreated through the forest.

When the last bluecoat was through the woods, Miles ordered his Pioneers to block the road high with fallen logs to prevent the enemy from using it for a new attack.

Once again General Sumner exclaimed, "Well done!" Miles was so weary this time that all he could manage was a smile.

That night McClellan ordered a general retreat to safer ground. He entrenched the Army of the Potomac southeast of the Southern capital, at Malvern Hill, and there on July 1 was attacked by General Lee. The Confederates were driven off, but McClellan retreated again instead of pressing his advantage. The siege of Richmond had been raised at last.

Now Nelson Miles learned a bitter lesson: a man might have military skill far above the average, unlimited personal courage in battle, and some influence, and still be cheated of his just reward.

General Sumner, a Bostonian, recommended Lieutenant Miles for promotion, placing his name at the head of the list. The governor of Massachusetts, however, had not forgotten and apparently had not forgiven the brash young man who had been so outspoken at the start of the war. He turned down Sumner's recommendation. There would be no promotion for Lieutenant Miles. It looked to Miles as though there never would be, no matter how gallant his deeds.

The governor of Massachusetts might play politics with Nelson Miles's military career, but there were men in the

Army of the Potomac who did have a high regard for him. Word of his exploits and his ability as a soldier spread.

Within weeks after his second rebuff from the Massachusetts State House, Colonel Francis C. Barlow of the 61st New York Volunteers called Miles to his headquarters tent and offered him the lieutenant colonelcy of the regiment.

Miles accepted on the spot. He would be sorry to leave General Sumner, for the two men had become close friends, but he much preferred the fighting part of war to staff work. In a few days the governor of New York granted him a commission as lieutenant colonel. He had jumped two grades in winning promotion. Nelson Miles had become the second in command at the age of 23!

The men of the 61st New York liked Miles. They discovered that he was firm, a strict disciplinarian, but that he was fair and considerate. His good nature helped. He had a way of getting men to do the impossible.

The thin, scholarly Barlow was wounded in the battle of Antietam September 16, 1862. Nelson Miles took over temporary command of the regiment. Not long afterward Barlow was promoted to brigadier general for gallantry in action, and Miles, still only 23, became colonel of the 61st New York.

The Federal troops fought Jackson and Stuart at Fredericksburg in December, 1862. The first day of battle started off with dense valley fog that lifted into bright sunshine. The objective was Marye's Heights, where the Rebels were entrenched behind a high stone wall. The

Union infantry charged, in close formation, into a withering enemy fire. The ranks were further decimated by bursting artillery shells.

Young Colonel Miles, at the head of the 61st, was in the hottest fire. "Come on! Follow me!" he shouted, waving his sword high over his head. Men of the 61st cheered and followed him on the double.

Then his men saw their colonel clutch his throat; his sword dropped. He reeled and was caught by two soldiers.

The blue-clad line charged up the hill, determined to be avenged. The two soldiers searched for a stretcher.

"Take me to General Howard," Miles ordered them as they placed him on the stretcher. Howard, his old commander, was back on duty again and now led the Second Division. Miles had a suggestion which he felt that he alone could make.

He was bleeding badly but he held the throat wound together with the fingers of one hand as best he could while the men trudged back to Howard's field headquarters.

Howard would have sent him to a field hospital at once, but Miles held up a protesting hand. He spoke in a thick voice, scarcely able to get the words out, but Howard understood his brief directions about where the Second Division should be placed to best advantage.

Howard knew his man. If Nelson Miles made a suggestion, it was sound. The general nodded in quick understanding, then ordered his friend sent to the nearest field hospital.

As at Fair Oaks, Miles's wonderful constitution pulled

him through, and within weeks he was back on duty. He intended to use the lull in the fighting during the cold winter months to make the 61st the best regiment in the division.

There was a long cease-fire during the winter of 1862-1863. It held from Virginia to the Rocky Mountains and from Ohio to the Gulf of Mexico. Men of the South sang "Dixie," "Bonnie Blue Flag," and other favorite war songs around their evening campfires. Only a few hundred yards away from Miles's regiment a Rebel outfit was bivouacked in full view of the Union troops. Not a shot was fired all winter, even when Miles's men sang "The Union Forever," "Battle Cry of Freedom," and "Tenting Tonight on the Old Camp Ground." Every night the men of both sides joined in singing "Home Sweet Home" in common bond of loneliness just before bugles sounded the sweet, melancholy notes of Taps. Miles's deep bass voice led the singing of his own men.

The Army of the Potomac had changed generals during the past year almost more often than its soldiers were able to change their shirts. By the spring of 1863 "Fighting Joe" Hooker was in command. Crossing the Rappahannock River, Hooker tangled with the Rebels. But he, too, failed to follow whatever advantage he might have won. Lee's army eluded him. Mr. Lincoln's generals seemed to have a habit of winning tactical victories but failing to follow them up.

A few days after the Rappahannock engagement,

"Stonewall" Jackson and his dashing cavalry leader, J. E. B. Stuart, led a daring raid to turn the Union flank at Chancellorsville. They caught Hooker napping, his men with their arms stacked.

The key army division holding the right flank was Howard's, in which Nelson Miles served with his 61st New York regiment. It was caught in the full fury of the Confederate assault. If his men fell back, there was danger that the whole Union right flank would crumble. Defeat of the flank could lead to what Lee had planned, a rolling up of Hooker's Army. With less than half as many men, Lee could wipe out or capture the whole Union Army. The war might be over right then!

Screeching and yelling, Southern troops came charging with fixed bayonets. Miles was proud of the way the men of the 61st New York met the charge. His long hours of drilling during the winter and his instruction in military tactics were paying off.

The Rebels were hurled back with steady rifle fire. There was no panic. The men behaved like the disciplined troops Miles had taught them to be, but there was no time for congratulations. Miles realized that flesh and blood and cold courage were not enough to stop the determined Rebels. And the Chancellorsville road had to be held at all costs!

Miles spotted a rise of ground nearby. It wasn't much of a hill, but it was thickly wooded, and there was wet ground in front of it. If he could hold off the Southern attack long enough to dig entrenchments and build a barricade of logs, perhaps he could control the road. The enemy would be forced to carry his earthworks before they could safely press on.

Some of the soldiers swapped rifles for axes and shovels. Pits were dug as other men felled trees and dragged the heavy logs forward to form an abatis, a barricade of trees with the branches pointing outward. Miles was careful to have his men sharpen the ends of the branches.

The men who dug the trenches and built the abatis were exposed to constant enemy fire. It was hard and dangerous work. Miles, heedless of his own safety, was everywhere, directing and encouraging the men.

The pits were dug deep and wide. The logs were securely fastened into position while the regiment kept up a steady drumfire on their attackers. At last the job was done.

To turn the Union flank now, Jackson's men would have to storm the man-made barrier on the Chancellorsville road under a withering fire. Some of them did try to carry the position, even jumping their horses over the logs, only to die under a hail of bullets.

But holding the road was not to be easy, even with the help of the effective barricade so hastily thrown up in front of the enemy. Success of the Southern flanking movement turned now on overcoming this hurdle. Waves of gray-uniformed men surged against the barrier for three days. Each assault broke on the volleys of lead poured into the attackers' ranks by Nelson Miles's men. Each time the Rebels charged they were hurled back with heavy losses.

Meanwhile, Hooker rushed reinforcements to the spot to bolster his right flank. Nelson Miles continued in command of the operation he had initiated. For three days he remained in the thick of the fighting, scarcely taking time for food, sleeping only in brief catnaps.

Steadily now the Rebels were losing. Worst of all for the Army of Northern Virginia, "Stonewall" Jackson himself was mortally wounded by one of his own soldiers, who mistook him for a Federal officer as he rode along the line of heaviest fighting. Lee would never win a decisive battle after he lost Jackson.

Riding along the line, encouraging his men to renewed effort as a new wave of gray-clad troops charged toward the breastworks, Miles was almost jolted from the saddle by the force of a blow near the pit of his stomach. A minié ball, deflected by the metal plate of his belt buckle, had pierced his left leg. Later he learned that his hipbone had been shattered, too, and that the pellet had lodged in his leg muscles.

At the moment he was intent only on forcing himself to remain upright in the saddle. It would not do for his men to know that he had been hit just when the Confederates were launching a new attack. Holding tightly with both hands to the pommel of his saddle to keep from falling, he turned his horse and walked the animal slowly toward the rear.

His head was swimming; he fought faintness, determined not to fall from the saddle. It took all of his strength of will, but he managed to keep himself on his horse. As though the animal knew its master had been badly wounded, it picked its way carefully and almost without guidance.

Outside a temporary field hospital Miles swung down from the saddle and was helped to a stretcher. It was many hours before he received attention. Then he was hauled in a bumpy wagon to a train and sent back to Washington and a hospital. Eventually, with the help of his older brother, Daniel, he was taken by train to his home in Westminster. There a doctor from Boston extracted the pellet and patched him up. Again, it was only because of his wonderfully strong constitution that he survived the wound and its delayed treatment.

Miles's holding action at the Chancellorsville road had saved the day for the Union Army. Lee's attempt to turn Hooker's right flank had failed. The Union Army of 130,000 men was safe. For his heroic act, Miles later received the Congressional Medal of Honor.

Lee now seemed to become overconfident despite his loss of Jackson. Soon he planned nothing less than an invasion of the North, perhaps even the capture of Washington. When the Federals realized what Lee intended, the Army of the Potomac under General George C. Meade hastily retreated across the Rappahannock, then over the Potomac, and prepared to defend Washington, Baltimore, and Philadelphia.

Instead of attacking the capital, however, Lee made a wide swing to the left, into Pennsylvania. He was stopped at the bloody battle of Gettysburg, July 1, 2, and 3, 1863.

Gettysburg has been called one of the eight decisive battles of the world, for it turned the tide of the war. Lee's army was crushed and forced to retreat south.

Nelson Miles missed this most important battle of the Civil War because of his almost-fatal wound at Chancellorsville, but not without making an attempt to get back into action. He tried, on crutches, to rejoin his regiment, but was ordered to the rear and told to report for duty only when he was completely well again.

He spent his time the next few months organizing a militia brigade to fight in the mountains of Pennsylvania. If Lee had won at Gettysburg and pressed on, Miles was prepared to harry the Rebels through the Pennsylvania hills. After those three terrible days at Gettysburg, however, the South was bled white. Lee retreated to Virginia, so Miles never got a chance to see what his new army could do.

Nelson returned to duty under the most happy circumstances. He was to serve under the command of a general with whom he shared a rule of warfare that had been applied successfully in many campaigns: "Always attack!"

While the Union armies in Virginia had been floundering from one poorly executed campaign to another, great events had been going forward in the western theater of war. General Ulysses Simpson Grant had conquered the western Confederacy from the Mississippi River to the Gulf of Mexico. Lincoln now brought Grant to the eastern front and made him supreme commander.

Grant was a West Pointer, and a rough-and-ready fighter. He believed there was just one way to defeat an enemy—get him on the run and keep him running until he couldn't run any farther and had to surrender. Either that or starve him out.

That was Nelson Miles's number one rule of warfare, too. He had fretted and fumed, sometimes not too tactfully, at the muddled campaigns in Virginia. He knew all about Grant's campaigns and his great victories in the West. Now he expected that there soon would be real results in the East.

Grant organized his new army from top to bottom for a drive to victory. It was a happy time for a young officer with Miles's high ambition and keen ability. Where Grant was, there was bound to be action, and Miles always found opportunity in action.

Grant crossed the Rapidan River in Virginia and began a great flanking movement on Lee's army defending Richmond. Grant fought through a heavily forested area known as the Wilderness, south of the Rapidan. So intense was the fire on both sides that the woods were burned and men were lucky to escape with no worse than scorched uniforms.

Lee had thrown up strong earthworks at Spotsylvania Courthouse, a little village some fifty-five miles northwest of Richmond. Grant wrote to General Halleck: "I propose to fight it out on this line, if it takes all summer." For many bloody days it seemed as though it might take even more than one summer to do the job.

The Rebel fire was terrific, so intense that minié balls cut down even standing trees. Miles saw one oak almost two feet in diameter felled by small-arms fire alone. The defenses were exceptionally strong. The Confederate earthworks were protected by heavy chevaux-de-frise, long, pointed wooden spikes placed at an angle to prevent assaulting troops from gaining the top of the earthen parapet.   1321667

On May 12, Grant ordered the earthworks taken by assault.

Nelson Miles, as usual, was in the thick of the fighting. He led his regiment against the barricade with fixed bayonets. Already the ground was so covered with dead men that those who followed had to walk on their bodies.

Miles saw that it would be impossible for his men to take the earthworks unless something drastic was done, and quickly. Every minute counted, for the enemy fire was intensified as the men of the 61st New York charged within range. There was just one way it might be done, but the risk was great.

He turned to his men, still advancing on the double behind him with bayonets fixed, and ordered them to tear out the spikes that protected the barricades. He knew that if enough of the wooden spikes could be pulled from the earthworks quickly he could clear a path over the top and into the trenches below.

Setting the example, Miles ran forward, sword in one hand, pistol in the other. As he ran he crouched low so that enemy troops could not shoot from the parapet without exposing themselves to fire from Union marksmen.

At the base of the earthworks he sheathed his sword and holstered his pistol. Miles seized the nearest wooden spike and motioned a brawny soldier nearby to help him. They pulled together. The spike came out much more easily than he had expected. The Rebels certainly must have thrown the earthworks loosely together, he thought.

The men of the 61st cheered as the first spike came out and was tossed to one side. Miles waved an arm, motioning for troops in the front ranks to help, then called to the others to maintain fire against the position to keep enemy defenders' heads down. Bullets from the weapons of his own men whistled over his head for the next few minutes as he helped pull out the spikes with his bare hands. As soon as a Rebel sharpshooter poked his head above the parapet, men of the blue line redoubled their fire. The firing became so heavy that few defenders were able to shoot at their attackers with accuracy.

Miles's hands were torn and bleeding, as were those of the men helping him, when he at last decided that the earthworks could be taken by storm without sacrificing the lives of too many men. He drew his sword again and, waving it high over his head, shouted, "Now, all together, boys! After them! Follow me!"

Over the top went the men of the 61st New York, Nelson Miles at their head. The Confederates renewed their heavy fire, but they were falling back now. Within minutes the fight became a hand-to-hand struggle, but the earthworks were captured. This time Miles was somewhat surprised to discover that he had escaped without a scratch, save for his bleeding hands.

Barlow was promoted to major general in command of a division, and Miles stepped into his shoes as brigadier general. Courage, initiative, and imagination, it seemed, were recognized on the field of battle if not by the politicians in Boston.

When Barlow became exhausted soon afterward in the hard fighting around Petersburg, not far from Richmond, Miles took over as acting commander. Again he rallied dispirited Union troops and turned the tide of battle. On August 25, 1864, he became brevet major general in permanent command of the First Division, the biggest division in the Army and the one that had suffered the heaviest casualties.

Some of the younger West Point officers were bitterly jealous, but they were forced to admit that Miles's promotion was deserved.

Grant and his Army of the Potomac now were hanging onto Lee's coattails "with bulldog tenacity," as Miles wrote home about the fighting, and the First Division was carrying a good part of Grant's load.

Casualties in the First Division were heavier than ever. There were not hours enough in the day for Nelson Miles to do all his work. A good division commander had to lead his troops by day and spend most of the night planning the next day's operations, attending staff meetings, and sitting in with the corps chief for briefings on the next day's orders. Yet Miles seemed tireless, perhaps because he loved his job—all except the necessary killing of men. The greater the responsibility, the more earnest the effort he put into it, and the greater satisfaction he got from it.

But he heartily wished that men of his own country were not his military enemies. He never thought of them as enemies personally, and often he pondered the problems his country would face once the war was ended and the tremendous task of reconstruction was begun. Never for a minute did he doubt that the Union would win.

Wonderful news came now from deeper in the South. General William Tecumseh Sherman had marched an army of 100,000 men from Chattanooga, Tennessee, to Atlanta, Georgia, and from Atlanta to Savannah, on the Atlantic coast. Sherman's army had not left enough food to keep a mouse alive. He had cut the Confederacy in two, just as Grant had sliced it down the middle in the West the year before.

Then Sherman marched north along the coast, carrying out that part of Grant's plan to end the war quickly. Off the Southern coast, grim United States warships and swift cruisers patrolled. They had shut off contraband shipments to the Confederacy from abroad. With few factories of their own and no other means of getting supplies or food, the South was not only being bled white in manpower on the battlefield, but also starved into submission by the tight sea blockade.

By March of 1865, Grant was ready for the final push. His army was closing in on Lee and Richmond.

Lee had little food for his men. Richmond was starving, and ammunition was running dangerously low. The Army of Northern Virginia, despite the high courage of the rank and file, was in low spirits.

Grant, on the other hand, had inspired his men of the Army of the Potomac to make one last great effort. He sent the Second Corps, in which Miles served as commander of the First Division, together with the Fifth Corps, to turn Lee's right flank. Lee countered swiftly, trying to roll up the Fifth's flank in turn.

Sensing danger, Miles swung his First Division suddenly to the left and attacked the Rebel line. So fiercely did his men fight that he drove the enemy from the field. The Fifth Corps, thus supported, rallied and with the help of the whole Second Corps drove the enemy still farther back. Miles's quick action had made the victory possible.

The war was drawing rapidly to an end. Grant's army was overpowering. Lee had been forced into one retreat after another. Even so, at Hatcher's Run, Miles's division tried three times under the cover of heavy timber and with the use of two batteries of field artillery before it was able to carry Rebel earthworks. The men of the South fought on stubbornly and bravely, still clinging to the faint hope that somehow Lee might achieve a victory for them.

The South was beaten and the men in gray knew it, but their courage was as fine as it had been during all of the four years of the war. Miles admired them for it, all the while pushing his own men day and night in relentless pursuit of victory.

Miles was intrigued by the way Grant drove his Army for the kill, never giving Lee a minute to regroup, pounding him day and night. As soon as Grant's cavalry could surround Lee and the Army could bring Union artillery up, the Army of Northern Virginia would be forced to surrender. Then the slaughter would end. Nelson Miles wanted that more than anything. He had said all along that Grant's kind of war could have cut the terrible casualties by ending the struggle sooner.

Richmond fell. President Lincoln entered the ruined city in sorrowful triumph. With the ragged and half-starved remnant of his Army of Northern Virginia, Lee retreated southwest to Appomattox. The gallant and brilliant leader of the South's principal military force was all but trapped at last.

As usual, Miles's men were leading the pursuit of Lee. On April 8, 1865, he saw a tall, thick column of dust. It could mean a wagon train, or retreating field artillery. On the dusty Virginia roads only a few wagons or wheels of mobile guns were needed to kick up a sizable cloud.

Miles ordered a detachment forward to reconnoiter. The general heard snatches of song as the men of the patrol slogged along in the growing heat at a steady pace. They, too, had seen the dust column. They were almost happy, for everyone realized that the war was nearly over; there was much speculation as to when the Rebels would surrender. Perhaps, they hoped, as their commander did, that there would be no more fighting. Most of them felt that if they lived through the next few days, they soon would be reunited with their loved ones at home.

The column of dust disturbed the general more than ever as he watched it rise higher into the sky and waited for a report from the scouting unit. The dust could mean fleeing wagons and artillery, but it might indicate that a part of Lee's army was attempting a flanking movement. If so, Miles had to be ready for it.

As he was about to spur forward himself, a blue-coated cavalryman, cap askew, galloped up, saluted, and reported sighting a very large wagon train with some artillery.

Miles rose in his saddle to look at the dust rising in a wide arc behind the present location of the wagon train. He wondered—then gave an order for a strong detachment of men to hurry forward in pursuit. It should not be difficult to capture a slow-moving wagon train.

Soon Miles heard the sharp crack of rifle fire ahead and knew that his men had engaged the defenders of the wagon train. He spurred forward, accompanied by his staff, and within minutes he watched the surrender of 250 vehicles and two pieces of field artillery. The thousand-man guard of the wagon train offered only token resistance.

"It's Jeff Davis's gold!" shouted men in the ranks. "It's the Confederate treasury!"

The wagons didn't carry gold, but they did contain what remained of the Confederate treasury. With Lee retreating, Richmond fallen, and the government of the Confederacy, including President Jefferson Davis, in flight, the paper money was worthless. There were millions of dollars of it. That night the men of the First Division had a good time playing poker for high stakes with Confederate currency. The general let them have their fun; it was good for the soldiers to relax after such a long period of hard fighting.

The next day Miles's division pursued the enemy along the Richmond-Lynchburg road toward Appomattox

Courthouse. General Philip H. Sheridan's cavalry had reached Appomattox Station, on the other side of the Confederate army, and during the day General Edward O. C. Ord's corps followed.

All day Miles listened for just one sound, the rolling thunder of Union guns on the other side of the Rebel lines. The sun was just setting when he heard the sweetest sound of four long years of war—the boom of cannon beyond Lee's retreating army.

Lee's army was surrounded. He could fight no more.

On April 9 a white flag of truce appeared from the enemy lines. Miles spurred forward to meet General Lee, who had come in person to ask Grant for a cease-fire while they talked terms of surrender.

Next to Grant, Lee had Miles's greatest admiration of all living military commanders, so it was with pride and sorrow that he took Lee's message. Grant was on the other side of the Army of Northern Virginia at the moment, conferring with Sheridan and Ord, but Miles promised to get Lee's message to him at once.

A meeting was arranged, and the Southern commander surrendered at Appomattox Courthouse a few hours later. His army had been reduced to fewer than 28,000 men.

Union cannon quickly thundered the glad tidings. Bands played "The Star Spangled Banner" and "Columbia." Men of both sides sang together and embraced each other for joy that the war had ended. There were still some Confederate units in the field, but the collapse of Lee's army meant that the war was over.

TWO

AFTER THE WAR—
YEARS OF PREPARATION

Brevet Major General Nelson Miles stood on the grim seaward parapet of Fortress Monroe at Old Point Comfort, Virginia, on a May morning in 1865.

The Civil War was over, the Confederacy overthrown, its officials either captured or in flight. Miles was a colonel in the Regular Army, with the brevet of major general. This was an honorary rank. He was entitled to be addressed as major general, but received the pay and subsistence of a colonel. He had won the assignment because of the ability and courage he had displayed on so many occasions during the war.

He saw a warship drop anchor in the harbor. Through

his field glass he could make out a boat being lowered away. On deck was a gaunt figure he recognized as Jefferson Davis, captured President of the Confederate States of America. Davis had been taken only a few days before and was on his way to Fortress Monroe as a common criminal. He was charged by the United States Government with being a plotter in the killing of President Abraham Lincoln on April 14, only a few days after Lee had surrendered.

General Grant himself had issued the order naming Nelson Miles commandant at Fortress Monroe—for one specific purpose: he was to become Jefferson Davis's jailer. His orders were to make absolutely certain that Davis did not escape. Grant had been much impressed by Miles's war record. He had picked him out of the entire Army for this all-important, if distasteful, job.

The country clamored for an immediate trial of Davis and the other suspected backers of John Wilkes Booth, the actor who had fired the fatal shot at Lincoln in Ford's Theater in Washington. There was a price of $100,000 on his head. Two years would pass before investigation disclosed that Davis had no part in the plot.

Miles felt none of the hatred for Jefferson Davis that was widespread in the country. He did not admire Davis as a man or as a Southern leader, but he was determined to treat him fairly and with as much consideration as his orders permitted. Nevertheless, he would make certain that Davis did not escape. Miles remembered the order he had just received from Charles A. Dana, Assistant Secretary of War. It read: "Brevet Major General Miles is hereby authorized and directed to place manacles and fetters upon the hands and feet of Jefferson Davis whenever he may deem it advisable in order to render imprisonment more secure."

Orders were orders, so when Jefferson Davis landed at Fortress Monroe Miles ordered him placed in irons. For weeks Miles personally supervised the delivery of every morsel of food, every item of clothing, and every other necessity to the prisoner. He made certain that no gun or knife or other weapon was smuggled in to Davis. The general stood outside the improvised iron-barred cell while Davis's pastor talked with the ex-President of the Confederacy. Even the minister was suspect when it came to weapons. Davis's wife was not allowed to visit him, for he was kept in solitary confinement.

Gradually Miles felt able to relax some of the severe restrictions on his prisoner. At the same time he tightened the safeguards against escape or rescue.

There were many persons in the South, and some in the North, who thought Miles was too strict in his guardianship of Davis. He felt he was as considerate as his orders permitted. His first duty was to his country.

Although Grant had allowed officers and men of the defeated Army of Northern Virginia to return home with their sidearms and horses, many of them, after a weary ride or walk, found very little with which to begin life anew. Plantations were weed-grown from neglect; houses were in ruins. Freed slaves either had fled or were living as squatters on land of their former masters, scarcely able to eke out a bare living. Many white families were in even worse condition than the Negroes. Many parts of the South that had been invaded by Union forces were desolate wastelands, and the South was without industry to which its workers could turn for a livelihood. Conditions were worse in the cities and larger towns. It would be almost a generation before recovery would be possible. The strong hand of the Federal Army was needed everywhere to begin the work of reconstruction.

The South was divided at once into military departments, districts, and divisions, with an army officer in command of each and with enough troops to preserve law and order. About a year after he was put in charge of Jefferson Davis, Miles was transferred from Fortress Monroe to the military district of Raleigh, North Carolina.

Miles was appalled at the plight in which he found the Negro population of North Carolina. He began at once to carry out a program of relief. He wrote to influential friends in Boston, New York, and Philadelphia and asked for huge quantities of clothing and other supplies for distribution to destitute Negroes of his district. Many people sent money, too. Then, in a report to the Federal government, he strongly urged the establishment of more schools as the quickest and most certain way of getting the Negro people on the road to good citizenship. He set up 250 schools himself while waiting for the government to act.

He served two years as military governor in the South, in North Carolina and in Virginia, obeying orders, but not

liking most of what he saw and some of what he had to
do as a soldier.

But it was not all work for Nelson Miles. He went to
Boston or to Westminster on leave. Now and then duty
called him to Washington, and he found time to relax in
the social life of the capital.

In army circles and in capital society there was much
talk about the good-looking young blond officer with the
drooping cavalry mustache. Somewhat stiff and ill at ease
at large parties, especially with women present, he was a
pleasant conversationalist and good company at small gath-
erings. No wonder feminine hearts fluttered when Miles
entered a drawing room or sat down at a formal dinner.
But he wasn't a ladies' man. He had been too poor, and
much too intent on making his way up in the world, to
pay much attention to young women.

Nelson Miles was one of the most promising young officers in the Regular Army, and General Sherman had his
eye on him. Miles had that military imagination, daring,
and relentless will which were so much a part of Sherman
himself. General Sherman was the brother of Senator John
Sherman of Ohio. When he was in Washington, General
Sherman was frequently a houseguest of the Senator. And
almost as often, their niece, vivacious Mary Hoyt Sherman, daughter of Judge Charles Sherman of Cleveland,
was also a guest of her uncle. Her father was a commis-
sioner of the then-building Union Pacific Railroad, and
his duties often called him to Washington.

When Miles met auburn-haired, blue-eyed Mary Sherman he fell deeply in love, almost at first sight. The feeling, he soon learned, was returned, and he was in the midst of a whirlwind courtship. They were married in Trinity Church, Cleveland, in June, 1868.

Within a year Miles was ordered to report at Fort Hays, Kansas, as commander of the Fifth Infantry. At last he was to get his long-cherished wish—to go West and fight Indians!

Miles felt a new exhilaration. At long last, after chafing at delay, he was to have his first command on the frontier. Marriage seemed to have made him more ambitious than ever. His new assignment gave him an opportunity to win new fame and promotion.

The couple stopped over at Fort Leavenworth during the winter months of 1868-1869. There was a round of social functions to welcome them, for most of the officers of the fighting regiments and the engineering service were in winter quarters. The fort was the biggest and most important post on the frontier. Great quantities of supplies, arms, and ammunition required by the Army for its almost continual war against the Indians were stored there; most of the expeditions, against the natives or to establish new forts in the wilderness, were outfitted at Leavenworth.

Miles and his bride could travel all but the last sixty-five miles by train; then they would ride overland to Fort Hays under military escort. Spring was the time of the year when the Indians took to the warpath after a long winter's rest in camp. There was danger every foot of the way over the open prairie, but Miles felt they would be safe enough with the soldiers to protect them.

Spring flowers colored the rolling Kansas prairie as Nelson and Mary Miles journeyed the two hundred miles from Fort Leavenworth to the railhead. A big herd of shaggy buffalo grazed quietly on the prairie. Frightened by the shriek of the whistle of the wood-burning locomotive, a big buck antelope cleared a thicket by the railroad right of way and bounded off into the shelter of the tall buffalo grass. Off to the right a herd of elk sought cover from the black monster that belched smoke and cinders and sometimes set fire to the prairie. Deer leaped clear of the tracks and fled. A covey of quail, frightened by the noise of the engine, arose from an island clump of prairie grass. They whirred high overhead and were quickly out of sight.

Later, as evening fell, wolves and coyotes skulked in the shadows. They were not too much afraid of the snorting monster that passed their secret hideaways; besides, it flushed out rabbits and other small game, making easier hunting. After dark both the wolves and the coyotes made the hours hideous with their howling. Those hours of the trip Mary detested.

She had seen and heard it all before. Twice she had gone with her father on western inspections of the Union Pacific. To Miles, however, the trip had been a series of eye-openers. It was new country for him, and as he began to feel its spaciousness and its vast opportunities, he thrilled to realize that he was at last to have a hand in its development.

Nelson Miles's fame had preceded him. The Fifth Infantry was a proud military organization; its officers were
some of the finest men in the Regular Army. All of them
were veterans of the Civil War, and some had seen years
of Indian fighting. The men in the ranks were also deeply
concerned that their new commanding officer should measure up to the best traditions of the outfit.

Officers and men of the cavalry escort which met the
train were not disappointed as Miles stepped down and
smartly returned their salute. As for the general's lady,
they seemed to like her, too. Mary Miles wore her auburn
hair well off a high forehead. Her blue eyes, set beneath
long lashes and thick brows, were at once steady and understanding, and her friendly smile came quickly. The
easy way she sat the sidesaddle as she nudged her horse
alongside the general's told the men all the rest they needed
to know. She might be new to the frontier, as was Miles
himself, but she was "army." They also liked her evident
affection for the two handsome hunting dogs Miles had
brought along with him to his prairie post.

Shortly before Fort Hays was sighted, the officer in
command of the escort column gave a low order to one
of the troopers. The man spurred forward and soon disappeared in a cloud of high-swirling dust.

Miles suspected the reason for the man's hurried departure, but Mary turned to him in quick concern. She was
fast learning that she would need more time than she had
thought to accustom herself to life in the vast wilderness,
with the possibility of savages lurking everywhere, day and
night.

"I suspect that our messenger is being sent ahead to warn the garrison of our approach. Prepare yourself for a formal dress parade of welcome," Miles said reassuringly.

By then they could see the sentries walking the high parapet along the stockade. The flag snapped in a light breeze. They heard a bugle sound the quick, imperative notes of assembly.

The big double gates swung slowly open as the cavalcade trotted toward the fort. Blue-clad sentries stepped smartly outside and presented arms. As the little column slowed to a walk through the gates, officers and men of the Fifth Infantry could be seen lined up in dress parade, all in their best uniforms. The blades of drawn swords and polished rifle barrels glistened in the sunlight. The regimental band played a lively martial tune. Nelson Miles and his wife rode slowly down the line, and he took the salute from the officer of the day.

That night there was a gala ball given by the officers and their wives for the new commanding officer and his lovely young wife. Every man was dressed in his best blue uniform with gold buttons and shoulder straps, and the women were gay in silk and satin. They, too, liked Mary.

The next day Miles plunged into the work of making the Fifth Infantry the finest and toughest on the frontier.

His wife set about making a home in the wilderness. Mary Miles had been reared in a comfortable home in Cleveland and was accustomed to the social life of Washington, but she readily adapted to the rugged life of a frontier army post. Perhaps that was one reason the women so quickly became fond of her.

She found that there were few conveniences such as a housewife knew back home. And very little furniture. She had to be content with the few pieces of silver and a favorite chair and table she had been able to bring along in the wagon train. The rest of her household equipment was makeshift, but with the help of the post carpenter and a little ingenuity she soon made her new home comfortable. There was a fireplace in the living room of their quarters, and it helped her to make the place attractive, even gracious, for the frontier.

To be sure, it was a nuisance that water for all purposes had to be hauled a quarter of a mile by wagon from Big Creek, a tributary of the Kansas River, and poured into barrels near the kitchen door. There were many other inconveniences, but she did have a good stove, and that was more than some of the wives had. Fortunately, at Fort Leavenworth Mary had been able to hire a cook who was not afraid to venture so far into Indian country.

Fortunately, too, she had a husband who was never fussy about either food or comfort. Whatever the day afforded was all right with Miles, for it was a part of the soldier's life that he loved.

Mary had brought along her "mess chest," as every army wife did. It could travel with her, even on the march. In the big, strongly bound box were six of everything for the table—knives, forks, spoons, cups, saucers, plates, and other dinner tableware; for the kitchen there were pots, frying pans, a carving knife and fork, and big spoons for stirring and serving. When there were to be more than six at table, she would have to do as other wives did—scurry along officers' row and borrow what she did not have.

Food was no real problem, she quickly discovered; buffalo and deer were hunted frequently. The hunting had to be done under strong military escort because of the danger from Indians, but the hunters didn't mind that. Small game birds were plentiful. The open prairie not far from the fort was a favorite feeding ground for quail and pheasant. When the hunters returned empty-handed, as they sometimes did, the post commissary always could provide ham or bacon, although more often than not they were a bit salty.

Obtaining eggs was a real problem for a housewife at Fort Hays. They could be had only at considerable expense and then only when some officer had business back in Fort Leavenworth. Usually just a few were intact at the end of the trip. And without eggs there could be no cake and no pudding, let alone eggs to go with bacon or ham for breakfast.

Not far from Fort Hays, on the open prairie, was the tented camp of the Seventh Cavalry. Only a small detachment of this famous outfit had been left behind as caretakers when Brevet Major General George Armstrong Custer had left on a winter campaign in Indian Territory. As always, Custer was accompanied by his wife, Libbie.

One day not long after Miles's arrival at Fort Hays, a scout rode in and reported to him that "Georgie" Custer and the Seventh Cavalry were returning to base. Within hours they would be back in camp. Custer was returning after victory over Black Kettle, a noted Cheyenne chief. In a pitched battle the troops had killed the chief, burned his village, and captured several braves and squaws whom they were returning to Fort Hays as hostages.

Miles's pulse quickened. He had been looking forward to a reunion with Custer. The two men had known each other since Civil War days when Miles led the infantry that spearheaded the last drive on Lee and Custer rode with Sheridan to surround the far side of the Confederate line.

Miles and Custer were of the same age, but of entirely different temperaments. They shared a love of hunting and outdoor life, of dogs and fast-paced horses, and of adventure and devotion to family. They also shared a calm courage that never stopped to consider personal safety and a capacity to make almost instant decisions in the heat of battle.

Some acquaintances said Custer was a bit of a show-off, but the same could never have been said of Nelson Miles. Custer liked to ride into battle in buckskin and a wide-brimmed hat rather than in army blue. Most of the time he wore his bright yellow hair down to his shoulders. He, too, affected a cavalry mustache. Miles somewhat envied Custer, who had preceded him on the frontier by almost two years and had ridden with Sheridan against the Sioux and the Cheyennes, the "dog-face people."

George Armstrong Custer's courage never had been questioned, and his judgment in military matters was seldom challenged. Custer, cavalryman and West Point graduate, and Miles, infantryman and volunteer, were rivals in the service and for promotion, but even their arguments over tactics never dampened the spirit of their friendship. It would be a real reunion for the two companions in arms, and Miles made plans at once for a rousing reception for his old friend and the gallant Seventh Cavalry.

Miles rode out to meet Custer as the band of the Fifth Infantry played the spirited strains of "Garry Owen," which was the favorite tune of the Seventh Cavalry.

So began an all too short period of friendly social contact. Libbie Custer and Mary Miles became fast friends from the first, and Mary considered herself fortunate to have someone who could teach her so much about army life on the frontier. She found Libbie Custer to be as charming as her magnetic husband.

When military business did not require their presence in the field, Miles and Custer often went hunting. They shot buffalo, which was a most exciting sport, usually from horseback. Sometimes it could be a dangerous sport, too. Each had several narrow escapes from being gored to death by wounded or enraged bulls. They hunted for antelope, elk, deer, or smaller game as well. Between them they kept not only their own larders but also those of many another officer in good supply of game.

Frequently the two couples spent the evening dining and visiting. It was on such occasions, with intimate friends, that Miles was at his social best. He could relax and talk about those things which interested him most.

The frontier was only temporarily quiet.

An expedition under General Eugene A. Carr of the

Fifth Cavalry surprised and attacked a large Indian camp on July 2 after a forced march. The troopers killed and wounded many natives. On September 17, a force of fifty frontier riflemen under Colonel George A. Forsythe was attacked by several hundred Indians while bivouacked on the Arikaree River. Colonel Forsythe drove them off after a nine-day siege. There were heavy losses on both sides. Forsythe lost half of his command before a rescue column arrived.

Although the Indians were decisively defeated in these and other encounters, they seemed to be more determined than ever to carry on their hit-and-run war.

"It is not enough to wait for the savages to attack at some isolated place and then send a column of troops dashing madly after them," Miles told Custer one evening as they sat around a cheery fire in Miles's big living room at Fort Hays. "As often as not the hostiles are so skilled at camouflage and escape that the troops fail to locate them."

Custer realized that he was a veteran of Indian fighting while Miles was a newcomer to the Plains, but he did not want to hurt his friend's feelings, and besides, he wanted to hear Miles's ideas. "And how do you propose, Nelson, to change our tactics?" he asked.

"I would use more scouts and I would improve our scout system by using more friendly Indians as spies," Miles explained. "And I would keep them near the reservations, where they could watch out for trouble. Then, when the hostiles took to the warpath, we could strike first. We should save lives all around that way."

Custer shrugged. He was not convinced. He had a low opinion of Indians as fighting men. "The Seventh Cavalry," he liked to boast, "can lick any number of Indians it meets—anywhere, any time."

Custer liked the limelight of fame, but he shared little of his friend's crusading spirit. He shook his head doubtfully. "It sounds good, Nelson, but I'm afraid you'll have a hard time convincing the higher-ups."

"That doesn't speak very well for their intelligence," snapped Miles. He knew from bitter experience that Custer was probably right. "But one day," he added, "we shall stop playing hide and seek with the savages and really do a good job of keeping them on their reservations. Then the frontier will be safe, and if we do our job right, the Indians will be fairly treated, and maybe we can civilize them."

Custer shrugged again. At the moment he was more interested in turning the conversation to the merits of his two new wolfhounds, just arrived from the East. They were handsome animals, and he was proud of them. The dogs were a topic which Miles could share with equal enthusiasm, for next to Mary and the Army, he loved horses and dogs. Since taking over at Fort Hays he had already acquired two fine chargers and two more hunting dogs. The dogs had the run of his quarters and were as much pets as hunters, for he liked to have them about in the little time he found to relax. Mary found that the beasts tracked in a great deal of dirt, especially in wet weather, but she liked the dogs, too, and anyway she would not spoil her husband's pleasure.

In the late autumn Custer was transferred to another post, and Mary went back to Cleveland to await the birth of her first child, a girl whom they named Cecelia.

Miles transferred his command to Fort Harker and then to Fort Leavenworth, where Mary joined him upon her return to the frontier with "little Cecelia," as Miles fondly called the baby. Mary liked Leavenworth, but their assignment there proved to be four years of frustration for Miles.

He was furious as he saw other men, some of whom had been of lower rank during the Civil War, promoted and given commands in the field, where they would have a chance to make names for themselves while he handled routine work at the base. He fumed at the application of the rule of seniority by which officers were usually promoted, regardless of merit.

Chief of the officers against whom Miles's spleen was vented was bearded Lieutenant Colonel George Crook, a West Pointer and, like Miles, a brevet major general. When Crook was promoted to the permanent rank of brigadier general and given an important command in New Mexico, Miles was particularly bitter. He felt that West Pointers were being favored, and he considered most of the officers so promoted, including Crook, far less able than himself. He was not reticent about telling General Sherman, now the General-in-Chief in Washington, of his disappointment and disapproval. He spoke not so much from jealousy as from a firm conviction that he could do the job better. Miles's opinion was not shared in Washington. Nor did Mary's pleas to her "Uncle Cump" in her husband's behalf bring results. Sherman was bending over backward not to seem to favor his nephew-in-law. He continued to take that attitude for many years. Besides, Sherman liked Crook and his military record.

What Miles bitterly called "inaction" nonetheless carried him into the field frequently between 1869 and 1874, but always in a subordinate capacity. Because of his burning ambition and bitter disappointment, Miles could not realize at the time that a long apprenticeship on the frontier was the best thing that could have happened to him. Just as five years of clerking in a crockery store had given him an appreciation of organization and paper work invaluable for an officer in the Army, and as his long staff work before getting a field command during the Civil War had given him a good understanding of headquarters work, so now his enforced inactivity at Fort Leavenworth gave him the time and the opportunity to learn much about Indians and the best methods of fighting them. During his years of administrative work, Miles profited by the mistakes of other officers, all of whose actions were reported and recorded at Fort Leavenworth, headquarters of the Department of the Missouri. Had he been in the field more often, he might have made some of the mistakes of the officers who had earlier chances than he at cleaning up the frontier.

While waiting for a field assignment, Miles learned the nature and the habits of the Indians and the different customs of the various tribes. He discovered which chiefs might be trusted and which ones were the bitter enemies of the white men no matter how much was done for their people.

He also learned how *not* to fight Indians and when to sympathize with them and help them. Already Miles had come to respect the natives, some of whose ways, he said, the white man might well adopt. He could admire the Indian's courage and fortitude and his ability in both strategy and tactics. He had a deep sympathy for the people who had been driven from one defensive position to another over the centuries. They were fighting for their lives and for their way of life; he loved his own freedom too much to deny that others had the same right. Yet he realized, too, that the Indians must be controlled if the white man's civilization was to continue its progress from the Atlantic to the Pacific, permitting the United States to become a great continental nation. If the Indians were controlled by force, however, they must be treated fairly. They must be provided with a place to live and taught the ways of agriculture. Then they might learn to live comfortably without hunting and roving over wide areas.

The Indian tribes were still being forced westward by the march of civilization. Behind the Union Pacific Railroad had come settlers, miners, trappers, hunters, and adventurers. Long wagon trains set out every spring from St. Louis, Missouri, Independence, Kansas, and other points for the Far West. Only a century before, the Sioux had hunted buffalo just west of the Great Lakes. Now they hunted on swift ponies with both bow and arrow and rifle as far west as Montana.

All the tribes were finding buffalo scarce. The great shaggy beasts had provided the chief supply of meat, clothing, shelter, and fuel for most of the natives. Not only buffalo, but also deer, elk, antelope, and smaller game, upon which the Indians depended for food, migrated to other regions. When the white men drove game westward, the Indians had to follow.

Conditions became rapidly worse near the end of 1873.

When it was discovered in the East that buffalo leather could be used as belting for machinery, the demand for hides shot up. Hunters by the hundreds began the wholesale slaughter of the great beasts. They invaded the vast areas of land given by solemn treaty to the Indians, and the Army did little to stop them. Hunting buffalo for hides to be used in Eastern industry had become big business, and the rights of the Indians were forgotten again. But this time breaking the treaty resulted in near starvation for the dispossessed people.

The Indians became desperate when their families starved during the long cold winters. Such expeditions as Sheridan's and Custer's had subdued them for a while, but the natives seemed more determined than ever to fight. They would not stay for long on their reservations.

Big war parties often gathered in Colorado, Texas, Kansas, and other territories. The warriors attacked surveying parties and workmen along the railroad right of way. Lonely homesteads and wagon trains were victims of their sudden massacres. Troops had to be available to move quickly, but even the establishment of more army posts did not help much.

It was evident that the Indians were getting a bigger supply of modern rifles and that they had become better shots at close range. When Colonel Joseph Fetterman's command of eighty officers and men was wiped out by Chief Red Cloud and young Chief Crazy Horse in 1867, only six of those killed in ambush were hit by Indian bullets. Arrows accounted for all the others. In only seven years it was the other way around. Miles was more convinced than ever that the Army must adopt new tactics.

At last Nelson Miles, who had been complaining so long to Sherman, was to get his chance. It seemed that at last he had worn down even Sherman's resistance.

Kiowa and Comanche lodges were bare of food. Women and children were starving in the winter of 1873-1874. Chiefs Graybeard and Stone Calf led their people from the reservations on what they meant to be a long, hard trek to New Mexico and Texas. There they hoped to find plenty of game and a safe refuge from buffalo hunters and white men who cheated, robbed, and murdered them. This time they would fight their way to a new land of plenty, with freedom to roam and to hunt as their forefathers had. Thousands of braves mounted war ponies, shiny new rifles in front of them, and squaws strapped draft ponies to the travois poles which would carry the tepees, cooking pots, and the few miserable belongings of each lodge into the wilderness.

For months traders, homesteaders, and merchants in towns in Oklahoma and Kansas had been demanding that the Army take measures to prevent just such an outbreak.

Now a new frontier war was threatened unless the natives could be rounded up quickly. They had to be driven back to their reservations and kept there.

During his years at Fort Leavenworth, Miles had been telling every superior officer who would listen to him of his plan to get the jump on the Indians the next time they took to the warpath. As a result, there was a somewhat better system in operation near the reservations for getting this information quickly back to headquarters. Miles worked hard to perfect his spy system, and it was particularly effective in the vicinity of the Indian Territory reservations occupied by Chiefs Graybeard and Stone Calf. Word was quickly sent to General John Pope, now commanding at Leavenworth, of the escape of the Kiowas and Comanches southward: they had broken out of Oklahoma and were believed to be heading for Texas and New Mexico. They would kill and loot, if they had to, in order to live.

Orders were received at Fort Leavenworth specifically assigning Miles to organize a column of cavalry and mounted infantry to pursue the Indians and bring them back to Indian Territory, as Oklahoma then was known. His command would consist of eight troops of cavalry, four companies of infantry, a company of friendly Delaware Indians, a detachment of artillery, and a company of civilian scouts and guides.

Three other commands were also ordered to take the field, with the idea of squeezing the Indians in from four sides. One command would move east from New Mexico, one west from Indian Territory, and one north from Texas.

Miles set out in August from Fort Dodge, Kansas, on the Arkansas River, confident but wary. He was determined to be the first to contact the "hostiles," as the Army called the Indians. It was his first really big chance since arriving on the frontier, and he did not want Crook, in command of the column from New Mexico, or any other rival officer, to deprive him of the honor and the glory this time! He might not be as colorful as some officers on the frontier, particularly those who knew how to get favorable publicity, but he knew he could do the job. Doing the job was not enough, it seemed, to get ahead in the frontier wars; an aspiring officer had to make a name for himself. Well, he could do that, too!

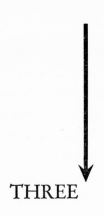

THREE

KIOWAS AND COMANCHES

NELSON MILES rode at the head of a long column of troops in the scorching sun of a late summer day. Sabers rattled as steel scabbards slapped against hard saddle leather. Harness leather creaked as men and animals, all in low spirits, plodded slowly through Oklahoma toward the Red River. There they hoped to find fresh water.

The dust was an enveloping shroud of hot, stifling, powdered earth kicked up by the horses in the long column that wound snakelike along a poorly defined trail. Men rode with big yellow or blue kerchiefs over the lower part of the face to keep out some of the dust. Others used the kerchiefs to cover the back of the neck. A thick film coated uniforms, hats, equipment, and animals—the accumulation of days of marching from Fort Dodge.

In all his soldiering Miles had never known such dust. It was fine, gritty, biting. It slid down his neck; it worked through his uniform blouse to his skin, through the tops of his long boots, seeping down to toe and heel; it dug into his sides; it coated the membranes of his nose and throat until he was so hoarse he seemed to croak when he gave an order; it threw up a screen so thick that at times he could see no more than a few hundred yards ahead. He desperately hoped the dust would not clog the barrels of the carbines of his cavalrymen or the rifles of his infantrymen. He had expected a dusty ride, but nothing like this.

It was the roughest and most desolate country he had seen since he arrived in the West. It was country that was hard on both horse and man. Even the hunting dogs he had brought along were suffering from the dust and lack of water.

Here was no lush land like the prairies of Kansas on which he had hunted with so much pleasure, with grass growing higher than the pommel of a saddle. Here were no great herds of buffalo to be shot for meat and hides at the will of either white man or Indian. There were no elk or antelope, nor even an occasional bear wandering far from its haunts in the distant mountains. There were no wild flowers.

Locusts had stripped the land almost bare of vegetation. It seemed there was not food enough to keep even a crow alive. Indeed, he had seen no birds since they left Kansas.

Miles sat his horse easily though wearily, his senses alert for danger, for they were in country where they might expect to find some of the thousands of hostile Indians his command had been sent to round up. The great cloud of dust kicked up by the horses surely would be seen by the keen-eyed scouts of Chief Graybeard and Chief Stone Calf.

Again Miles thought of the many things which five years on the frontier had taught him about Indians. He expected that the two chiefs would fight to the last man before they would abandon their march to new hunting grounds. If there were only some way by which he could persuade them to return to their reservations in Oklahoma without a fight.

Already the fleeing savages were killing and burning. Miles heard of a family of Georgians named Germaine who had been on the way from Missouri to Colorado as home-steaders. They had been attacked in Oklahoma. John Germaine had been killed, with his wife and several children, while defending his lone wagon train. Two small girls were taken captive by Chief Graybeard and two older girls had disappeared with Chief Stone Calf's band. Miles was determined to rescue all four of the girls if he could. Indians usually killed their captives when attacked, however, so the chances of saving the girls were none too good.

He could not blame the fleeing Indians too much for having broken out of their reservations. After all, the Indians of Oklahoma were part of a race which had been free to roam and to hunt some 600,000 square miles of territory unmolested until quite recently. Then they had been restricted to narrow quarters on reservations, but even the reservations had been invaded by greedy white men in the quest for buffalo hides. Now the tribes were seeking a new home, and they would fight any force which tried to stop them. Would he, in their place, do less?

Miles was proud of his first big field command on the frontier, and he had no fear of its reaction in battle. Before they left Fort Dodge he had instilled a simple rule into every officer and enlisted man: "Never, by day or by night, permit the command to be surprised by the enemy. Always be ready to fight. Keep in communication and support, and always act on the offensive."

Too many good officers and men had been killed on the frontier in the past because they had become careless. All too often they had been contemptuous of the Indian as a mere savage and a cowardly warrior.

Miles had another rule: "When you see Indians, be careful; when you do not see them, be more careful."

He was thinking now of those two rules by which an army command in Indian country might hope to stay alive. In such a landscape as this, where every boulder, every bit of sagebrush, every arroyo, every narrow passage, every depression in the ground might hide a warrior lying in ambush, observance of the precautions was even more necessary.

Up ahead as the dust lifted a bit, he could see his company of scouts under Lieutenant Frank D. Baldwin. His heart warmed as the solid figure of his chief of scouts

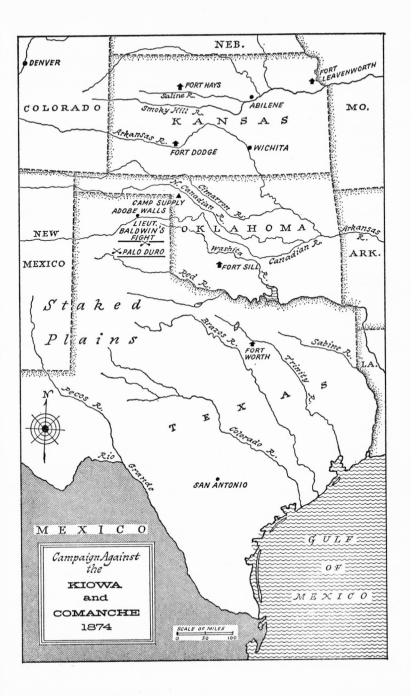

NEB.

DENVER

FORT LEAVENWORTH

COLORADO

FORT HAYS

Saline R.

Smoky Hill R.

ABILENE

MO.

K A N S A S

Arkansas R.

FORT DODGE

WICHITA

N. Canadian R.

Cimarron R.

CAMP SUPPLY
ADOBE WALLS

O K L A H O M A

Arkansas R.

NEW

LIEUT.
BALDWIN'S
FIGHT

PALO DURO

Washita

Canadian R.

ARK.

MEXICO

FORT SILL

Red R.

S t a k e d

Brazos R.

Sabine R.

P l a i n s

FORT
WORTH

Trinity R.

LA.

N

Pecos R.

T
E
X
A
S

Colorado R.

Rio Grande

SAN ANTONIO

M E X I C O

Campaign Against
the

KIOWA
and
COMANCHE
1874

G U L F

O F

M E X I C O

SCALE OF MILES
0   50   100

loomed briefly into view. How well Frank Baldwin always rode his horse. It was as though he were a part of horse and saddle. The swarthy, thickset ex-volunteer was a good man and there was none in the command in whom the general had greater confidence.

Already on this march, Baldwin had shown courage and resourcefulness which were the equal of his commander's. Miles had sent Baldwin and a force of about a hundred men on a flanking movement to the right of the column, to a place called Adobe Walls, the site of a recent Indian attack. Baldwin had flushed a band of escaping savages there and, instead of making a frontal assault or waiting to flank them, had sent his wagon train charging into the Indian camp. Taken by surprise, the hostiles had been routed and had fled. Then Baldwin rejoined the main column to take his place again in command of the advance force.

With Baldwin rode such noted scouts as Amos Chapman, who had a Cheyenne wife, and William Schmalsle. But Scout Ben Clark rode beside the general, his eyes seeming to take in the entire landscape at every glance despite the discomfort and the dust.

On the flanks of the column rode outposts of Indians and guides, alert for any sign of hostiles as the long column plodded over the parched ground. A horse snorted, trying to clear the dust from its nose; again saddle leather creaked; a wagon axle screeched. It would have to be attended to at the next brief stop.

The sun beat down hotter than ever.

Major C. E. Compton and Major James Biddle of the cavalry spurred forward to confer briefly with Miles, then fell back to their respective commands. Lieutenant James Pope, in charge of the artillery, sent a man forward to ask instructions for posting the guns at the next bivouac.

For an hour Miles had been uneasy. Common sense told him that no Indian in his right mind would linger in such open, undefendable country to make a sustained attack on the column. Anyway, it was well known that Indians seldom hit such a sizable body of troops, even on the march. True, Miles had only about half as many men for his expedition as the War Department had assigned to Crook for his task in New Mexico, and Miles's equipment lacked many essentials. He didn't have enough wagons to carry them. But a force of nearly 800 men was comparatively strong, even against the thousands of warriors in the Kiowa and Comanche group. It would be much better for the Indians to wait until the command had crossed the Red River into the Llano Estacado, or Staked Plains, in Texas and New Mexico to make an attack.

But common sense was no rule to go on in dealing with Indians. These fleeing tribes were desperate. Chief Graybeard and Chief Stone Calf must know by this time that a heavy column of troops was in hot pursuit. It would be instinctive for them to strike while the Army was moving and supposedly less defensible against surprise attack. The chiefs might or might not know that three other columns of troops were in the process of closing in from other directions.

"We must be near those big bluffs by the Red River that you told me about," Miles said, turning to Ben Clark.

The scout never took his eyes from the trail and the country on either side. He seemed to be searching behind every boulder and every clump of sagebrush. "Yes, sir. Quite near," he said.

Miles turned to the young orderly who rode on his other side. "Ride forward and present my compliments to Lieutenant Baldwin. Suggest to him that he throw out more flankers and an extra scout detail ahead of the column. We are nearing the Red River and may encounter hostiles at any moment." The orderly saluted and urged his tired mount forward to deliver the message.

Before he had ridden far there came the sharp crack of rifle fire, well ahead, and the war cry of Indians.

Ben Clark commented in a matter-of-fact voice, "Kiowas and Comanches. It's an ambush."

Miles turned in his saddle, arm uplifted. His sharp command, "Column halt!" could not be heard above the increasing din, but the hand signal served his purpose better than the vocal order.

The column ground to a halt as the junior officers and sergeants sharply repeated the order. Instinctively men fingered their weapons. They loosened sabers in scabbards; carbines were unbooted and the dust blown off. The men needed no orders for quick preparations for battle.

An aide spurred forward to Miles and saluted. "Send in the cavalry," the general ordered. "Compton and Biddle are to fight on foot if we are attacked in force. Pope will bring up the Gatling guns. Have them loaded and ready to fire."

Then Miles himself rode forward, Ben Clark at his side. The general found that Lieutenant Baldwin had dismounted his men to fight on foot at the first hostile shot. They had taken what cover they could. The soldiers and scouts were spread out in extended order, a dozen or more feet apart, so that each man presented less of a target. Horseholders were leading the riderless mounts to such safety as was available.

Gunsmoke combined with dust to choke both men and animals. The nearly naked Kiowas and Comanches were attacking from the yellow river bluffs onto the plain "with the fury of a whirlwind," as Miles wrote later, but they dared not completely encircle the men of the advance guard for fear of the troops farther to the rear. They could not run the risk of getting between two fires. All this Miles took in at a glance as he dismounted and crouched in a little arroyo beside Baldwin.

Then came the thunder of hoofs as a troop of the Sixth Cavalry rode up. Miles saw Captain Adna R. Chaffee's men, carbines blazing as they rode. The troop tore into the formation of mounted warriors. Chaffee waved his hat and shouted. Then his right fist pumped hard toward the right, the signal to "dismount, fight on foot, action right!"

Men slid from their horses, carbines in hand. They dropped to the ground and knelt to fire from the outside of a widening circle that was almost a hollow square, while horseholders led their mounts to the rear. They found shelter where they could behind scattered rocks and boulders in small ravines.

A second troop of cavalry thundered up and ground to a dust-choked halt. Before their captain could give the order to dismount and fight on foot, Miles was out of the arroyo. He sprang to the back of his own horse and drew his heavy saber. He waved it high over his head. "Follow me!"

Miles led the troop in a quick countercharge on the flank of the encircling hostiles. Men fired from the saddle or slashed with their sabers. The ragged fire of the Indians quickly lessened, then fell off to an occasional rifle crack as the troopers charged head on against the enemy flank. Caught between the advance guard of scouts and their supporting cavalry, and the charging troopers led by Miles, the hostiles quickly broke off the action and fled south toward the distant yellow bluffs.

It was all over within minutes, but in that brief time Lieutenant Pope had brought up his Gatling guns and brought them to bear. Now they would not be needed; the Indians were out of range.

The Gatling gun, or "coffee grinder," was a multi-barreled weapon fired by cranking. Slow and cumbersome by modern standards, it enabled the military of that day to pour fire at the enemy more rapidly than any other weapon.

Miles turned to his bugler, who had followed him into the thick of the battle. "Sound recall," he ordered.

The sweet, long notes of recall filled the dusty air.

Troopers turned their mounts about and trotted back to the scene of heaviest fighting. Already men of Chaffee's dismounted troops were remounting, booting their smoking carbines, and Baldwin was re-forming his advance guard.

"We'll give them a good run for their money," said Miles. He picked the troop that had encircled the hostiles to go in pursuit. "But be careful," he warned the young troop commander. "We can be sure that this band was only one small part of the main body. Don't be lured into an ambush."

The column re-formed and proceeded on its dusty march while the lone cavalry troop pushed ahead, chasing the hostiles over sand hills, over bluffs, through dry arroyos and coulees, more than twenty miles across the Red River and onto the Llano Estacado.

At the bluff-guarded edge of the Staked Plains, the troop turned back to the river. But already they knew what the rest of Miles's command soon would discover. The Red River, on which they had counted so much during the thirsty hours of their long march, was almost dry. What water there was, was found to be alkaline. It was not fit to drink.

The Llano Estacado, or Staked Plains, was a high, arid plateau in northwest Texas and southeast New Mexico. It stretched 400 miles north to south and 150 miles east to west. It was separated from the Rocky Mountains by the Pecos River. So much his scouts told Nelson Miles when his horse stumbled into the all but dry Red River.

The animal snuffled the alkaline water, which it could not drink, then snorted to clear its nose of the unsavory liquid.

Ben Clark, and soon other scouts and their Indian allies, scaled the bluffs that led onto the Staked Plains. The trail of the fleeing Indians was plain enough, and it led straight across the desert.

Now Miles knew for sure where the main body of Indians was headed. If they made it over the Llano Estacado, they would cross the Pecos in New Mexico and go into winter camp in the foothills of the mountains beyond. There, his scouts told him, they would find tree forage for their horses and ponies—not enough, but sufficient to keep the animals alive.

There would be some game in the hills and on the lower slopes, a few deer, some elk and antelope, perhaps a bear now and then, and plenty of partridge and rabbit. If the natives could keep from freezing to death in the fiercely cold winds that swept down from the heights and all the way across the Staked Plains, they might hope to come through the winter with minimum losses.

Miles had reason to believe from the reports of other scouts, however, that smaller bands of tribesmen, one of them under Chief Graybeard, had taken another route and were somewhere near McClellan Creek in the Texas panhandle. There were also other Indians loose in western Texas and southern Oklahoma. It was his job to round them all up and send them back to their agencies. He hoped one of the other three columns did not reach them first, for he very much wanted the honor of cleaning up the area by himself. What should he do? Try to follow Chief Stone Calf and the principal band across the Staked Plains, or send out detachments to locate and defeat the roving bands that apparently were still reluctant to go as far as Stone Calf was taking his people?

Miles decided his first duty was to try to cross the Staked Plains after Chief Stone Calf. But what lay between the Red River and the Pecos, across that vast wasteland? What dangers would his command encounter in pursuing the Indians across a country which his scouts told Miles resembled nothing so much as the great steppes of Russian Siberia?

There was no vegetation but short buffalo grass; no trees, no shrubs, no shade of any kind sheltered man or beast from the hot sun of summer or the terrible Texas northers that swept from the Rocky Mountains across the open plains in winter.

There would be little food except what was carried overland by wagon train from Camp Supply in northern Oklahoma or a nearer base camp that had been established on the Washita River, farther north. There was almost no game in the Staked Plains, his scouts told him—no deer, elk, or antelope. Rabbits and small game birds were almost as scarce.

More important than any other consideration was the fact that there would be little drinkable water on the long march across the Llano Estacado. Troops who followed the trail would have to carry their own water. With luck the horses could get along on what might be available. Even for those who did not take up active pursuit of the savages, there would be no water except the tasteless kind to be found in occasional and widely separated lagoons. Not until the fall rains, happily not too far away, would there be enough water in the Red River itself to provide an adequate supply for Miles's command.

The column scaled the yellow bluffs to the Plains and pushed on for days. As he had foreseen, they had little food and almost no water except what they carried. At last Miles dared risk the fate of men and animals no longer. Daily he was marching farther from his base of supplies. The Indian trail was plain enough. The hostiles were indeed headed for the Pecos and then for the foothills of the Rockies beyond the river.

Feeling almost as though he had failed in his first big mission, he reluctantly gave the order to face about and trek to somewhat more hospitable country. Winter came early, and he could not afford to be caught unprepared.

Then he came to another decision. He would make his wagon train a mobile base of supplies and the center of a roving winter cantonment. Thus he could keep a safe base within reasonable distance of fresh supplies and of field expeditions which he would send out in pursuit of Indians whenever and wherever a band was located. They would be forced to surrender and return to their agencies. If some should escape capture, he would harry them westward toward the Pecos, some 150 miles away. Once across that barrier the Indians would be hemmed in between the river and the mountains. If they were not starved into surrender during the winter, he could make a forced march across the Plains early in the spring. Meanwhile, he would concentrate on rounding up the bands still roaming Oklahoma and upper Texas. Some of them were believed to have gone into winter camp already.

Miles sent a strongly escorted wagon train back to Camp Supply for more of everything the command needed. Meanwhile, he constructed a log hut cantonment for his men and ordered warm clothing from Fort Leavenworth. He was certain the troops, warmly clad, could fight even in the extreme cold of a northwestern Texas winter.

It was the custom of troops campaigning against the Indians to go into winter quarters soon after the first snowfall, but he had other ideas. He planned to put into effect his principal rule of warfare: always attack. The rule had worked for Grant in the last days of the Civil War. It would work now against Graybeard and the lesser chiefs whose bands still roamed upper Texas and Oklahoma—if he could keep his soldiers in the field all winter.

Some weeks after the temporary camp had been set up, and as Miles was running low on supplies again with winter closing in fast, a dispatch came from the north that Graybeard was camped on McClellan Creek. Miles came to a quick decision. He summoned Lieutenant Frank Baldwin and told him to take wagons, scouts, a troop of cavalry, and a company of infantry for escort and proceed the next morning to the supply base on the Washita. If Baldwin could surprise Graybeard or any other band, he was to attack if he thought wise. The primary responsibility of the expedition, however, was to get supplies back to camp before snowfall. "Keep your eyes peeled for those two little Germaine girls Graybeard is holding captive," Miles added.

Baldwin's expression was as grim as his commander's as he replied, "I had them in mind, sir. I think that if I meet up with Graybeard, we shall attack."

Miles knew that the venture was in good hands. He was cheered, too, by information that another column of cavalry had captured a big band of Indians in New Mexico. The column that had been advancing from that area toward his would turn back now. Chief Big Tree and several other lesser chiefs also had surrendered, some of them going to Fort Sill, Oklahoma, but many Indians yet remained to be rounded up. It might take most of the winter to do the job.

Dawn was just breaking on the fourth day of Baldwin's march to the Washita River supply base when Scout W. F. Schmalsle galloped up to the campsite near a ridge overlooking McClellan Creek. He ground his horse to a spark-striking halt before Baldwin and reported that Graybeard's camp was over the hill.

Baldwin had just broken camp and the column was moving when the scout reported. Within a few minutes they might have stumbled into the camp quite unaware of it.

The young commander's right hand shot automatically

into the air, palm out, the signal for the column of wagons, cavalry, and infantry to halt. "How do you know it is Graybeard's camp?" he asked.

The scout grinned. "I've been in this country long enough to know Graybeard's tepee when I see it. There must be a hundred lodges down there," he added.

Baldwin knew that a hundred lodges meant three times that many warriors. The army expedition was far outnumbered. The wise thing would be to circle the camp, send back for reinforcements, and wait for them. Or go on to the Washita and forget Graybeard. But there were those two little girls.

Baldwin made his decision and proceeded to carry it out. The Indians might outnumber his command, but he had the advantage of surprise. He believed he had a way to stampede them. Once he got them on the run the rest should be easy. "Ride back to General Miles and tell him we are attacking Graybeard's camp!" he ordered the scout firmly.

Baldwin climbed to the top of the hill to have a look for himself and to plan his attack. Sure enough, there were at least a hundred lodges along the winding creek. Beyond was the prairie. The water and good forage were the reasons Graybeard had decided to remain on this spot for the winter instead of following Stone Calf across the Llano Estacado. There would be hunting, not good—for the white man had driven most of the game away—but enough to keep his people alive. He had only two other choices: to make the long, dangerous trip across the Staked Plains with winter setting in, or to return to his agency in Oklahoma and surrender his ponies and weapons.

Quickly Baldwin arranged for a surprise attack. Dawn would come soon and the Indian camp would be stirring. He had to hit it before it was fully awake. The command was formed in a double column, the wagons abreast of the cavalry. Infantrymen with rifles held at the ready were loaded into the wagons and supplied with plenty of ammunition. More cavalry was deployed to the right and left.

The columns pulled up the hill, reached its crest. Down below those in the forefront could see the sleeping Indian village. Not even a dog barked. At Baldwin's "Now!" the short, imperative notes of the charge sounded on the frosty morning air. The bugle call was the first warning that Graybeard and his village had that there was an enemy within rifle range.

Down the hill rolled the wagons, loaded with riflemen. The cavalry, carbines cracking, charged at full tilt, the troopers shouting at the top of their lungs. Wagonmasters lashed their mules to greater speed as they jolted over the rocks, sometimes nearly upsetting the vehicles. Cavalry horses struck sparks as shoes hit stones. Rifles cracked and pistols barked as the cavalcade swept into and through the camp.

Surprised and confused at the sudden attack at first, Graybeard quickly rallied his warriors. Many of them rushed out of their lodges nearly naked. The Indians made as much of a stand as they could in the open, but Baldwin's strategy had worked.

Tepees were knocked over; some were set on fire as the dry hides ignited in the embers of low campfires. Squaws and children hid where they could as bullets flew thicker than bees from an angry hive.

Horses screamed. Indian ponies broke their rawhide tethers and fled across McClellan Creek onto the rolling prairie. Indian braves ran after them, intent now only on regaining the mounts and making a stand against the troops farther on.

Graybeard himself escaped the first charge, but Baldwin's wagon-borne infantry and the cavalry pursued. Time after time the chief rallied his braves and made a stand behind some hillock or in a grove of trees, but each time the troops attacked again. Slowly the Indian band was being wiped out or split up. After four hours there were almost no savages in sight. Baldwin ordered his bugler to sound recall. It was time to attend to the second half of his business on McClellan Creek.

Baldwin found only old men, squaws, and crying children when he returned to the shattered camp. In one of the foul-smelling tepees he discovered Julia and Adelaide Germaine. One was seven, the other nine. They were almost naked despite the freezing weather, and they were terribly thin. The children's faces were pinched by starvation and their hands looked like bird claws. Already, it seemed, Graybeard's band was beginning to feel the effects of lack of sufficient food. They had none to waste on captives.

The little girls were overjoyed when they realized that their rescuers were army men. Baldwin made them as comfortable as he could. Troopers wrapped them in saddle roll blankets. Food and water were given to them, but sparingly, for the next few hours at frequent intervals. When they were finally able to talk the girls sobbed out a tragic story.

Their family had been on the way to Colorado after a stop in Missouri. Graybeard and Stone Calf had attacked their small party traveling alone in a covered wagon. Their father and mother and eldest sister, Jane, were killed in the fighting. The girls said that two other sisters, both older, were being held by Chief Stone Calf. What had happened to them Julia and Adelaide didn't know.

Julia and Adelaide told Baldwin they had been forced to do heavy work beyond their strength from the first. They had been fed just enough food and water to keep them alive. When winter set in, and as food became scarce, the little girls had been reduced to a few mouthfuls of food a day. They were scarcely able to move when the soldiers found them, and they talked only with considerable effort. Baldwin thought they probably would have died within a few days.

Two days later, after a forced march, Miles came thundering up at the head of a troop of cavalry. He found the Indian camp burned and the captives ready to be returned to their agency in Oklahoma. If Graybeard still wanted to defy the government, he and his warriors would have to live in the wilds for the winter without tepees, ponies, or supplies. Graybeard had been decisively defeated, and Miles had little doubt that soon he would return to the agency and surrender. The chief could not hope to join Stone Calf beyond the Pecos now.

"I shall recommend you for the Medal of Honor," Miles told Baldwin when he received the young officer's report. Miles did make the recommendation (Baldwin later received the medal, the highest military award of the United States Government), but the commander's first interest was for the little girls. He treated them as tenderly as though they were his own daughters, then sent them to Fort Leavenworth with Baldwin. With the girls went a note to Mary asking her to see that they received the best of care. Dr. Powell, the field surgeon attached to his command, was placed in charge of the girls for the journey. The troops needed a doctor with them, but the little girls, Miles felt, needed him more.

Miles had expected to keep his whole command in the field all winter. Now General Pope refused permission. Most of the men and equipment had to be sent back to Fort Leavenworth for the winter. Reluctantly Pope permitted a few troops to remain in the field for scouting in Texas and Oklahoma. All his life Miles had made disappointments pay dividends. He did not intend to be cheated of the chance to round up the rest of the Indians in the area just because his superior lacked his drive and imagination. Even with only a few men, Miles was determined to rid the area of hostiles before spring. To do less would be to fail in his mission in his own opinion, no matter what his orders were. "Scouting" could be made to cover a great deal more than General Pope might have thought.

Miles began a series of forced marches from one area to another, wherever he had reports of a band of Indians. Many of the hostiles were forced to surrender. They agreed to return to their agencies gladly enough, for now winter had come to the region.

The soldiers, outfitted in heavy wool and furs, nevertheless suffered from the severe cold. Some, including the general himself, froze their ears, fingers, or toes. The temperature sank to twenty-five degrees below zero some nights. Trying to sleep in blizzard-lashed tents was a nightmare. Miles's soldiers were accustomed to bitter hardship in the field, however, and there was no complaining. Many days the men sang as they marched through driving snow. Their commanding officer worked longer hours and got less sleep than any of them; he shared the same food. Thanks to his high spirits and the personal care he took to see that each man was as well equipped as circumstances permitted, the men kept their courage high.

Well along in January, Dr. Powell, the field surgeon, returned from Fort Leavenworth by way of Camp Supply and the quartermaster camp on the Washita River. He brought with him a photograph of Julia and Adelaide Germaine. The girls now looked well and strong, thanks to Mary's care, and they were smiling.

Miles decided to send the photograph secretly by a trusted Indian runner to the camp of Chief Stone Calf in the mountains beyond the Pecos. The runner would find the older Germaine girls and give it to them. Miles called an aide and dictated a letter.

Headquarters Indian Territory Expedition
In the Field, January 20th, 1875

To the Misses Germaine—

Your little sisters are well and in the hands of friends. Do not be discouraged. Every effort is being made for your welfare.

(Signed) Nelson A. Miles,
Colonel and Brevet Major General,
United States Army,
Commanding Expedition.

He indicated that the letter was to be copied at once, then turned back to Dr. Powell. "Already I have sent some of our friendly Indians to Stone Calf demanding his surrender. By this runner I shall send word that if he decides to accept my offer of surrender and return to the agency in Indian Territory, he first must agree to release the girls in good health, though what horrors they have undergone already I can only leave to your imagination. It makes my blood boil to think of it."

The cold-blooded Miles of the battlefield, with a quick eye for the tactical advantage, was an entirely different man when it came to the suffering of others. Even more than the desire to round up stray Indian bands in Indian Territory and upper Texas, the plight of the kidnapped girls had kept him in the field in such bitter weather. The men knew it, and they respected him all the more for it.

Within the hour the Indian runner was on his way. He would travel more than 150 miles across the Staked Plains in deep snow, in raging blizzards, over frozen rivers, and then across the Pecos to reach the main Indian camp in the foothills of the Rockies. After delivering his message to Chief Stone Calf, he would await a favorable chance to hand the letter and photograph secretly to the captive girls if they still lived. Miles had no doubt the runner would be able to make the journey and to carry out his secret mission. His friendly Indians were accustomed to making swift journeys on foot and to enduring extreme hardship the year around.

Stone Calf's band was suffering greatly from the cold. They were not equipped to face Texas northers in the buffalo hide tepees. Most of their horses had died of starvation. Their ponies, a tougher breed, had fared somewhat better, but they were too weak, and there were too few of them, to carry the band to a more favorable campsite even when spring came. Starvation faced the band before then, for there were no buffalo and little other game. Stone Calf accepted Miles's terms of surrender and hurried to give the hostages good treatment from then on.

Under the watchful eyes of a small detachment of troops, the band trekked back to their agencies in Indian Territory. It was a slow and painful march, and some of the band died on the way. Once back at the agency Stone Calf surrendered arms, ammunition, ponies, and the girls to the Indian agents.

Thanks to Miles's strong plea, the government set aside $10,000 of Indian funds as a trust for the four girls. For years the general took a personal interest in them, doing all he could for the sisters.

Graybeard and the stragglers of his routed band surrendered to their agency during the winter. Later the chief
was shot and killed trying to escape while under armed
escort to exile in a Florida Indian camp.

All the hostiles were safely back on their reservations
or agencies. Miles's winter campaign with only a few men
had cleared Colorado, Oklahoma, Texas, and New Mexico.
The vast area south of the Kansas line to the Red River and
west to the Pecos was at peace. Mary, Nelson, and little
Cecelia were reunited at Fort Leavenworth.

There was temporary peace on the frontier, but the
plight of the Indians who had been forced back to their
reservations was terrible. Miles protested, but not with
much success, when he found that many of the natives
were forced to live on scraps. Beef was supposed to take
the place of the buffalo which the agency Indians no longer
were permitted to hunt. Contractors were supplying poor
beef, unfit to eat.

All during his career on the Indian frontier Miles waged
an almost-constant war on dishonest contractors and timid
Indian agents. Whenever he could he appointed trusted
military officers to supervise the natives. He knew that
shabby treatment by the white man was the cause of most
Indian outrages which it was his duty to suppress. Miles
wondered how long it would be until another Indian outbreak would come.

Peace lasted on the frontier only until the autumn of
1875. Miles was ordered hurriedly to Cimarron, New Mexico, where he took command of a strong detachment of

cavalry. He could have attacked the warring Indians in their camps, as some other officers had done to other tribes, but that was not his way. Always he preferred to make peace with the natives rather than fight them, for he knew they always lost in the long run, and he felt there were always two sides to every story. He sent for the chiefs of the Jacarillas and the Muaches. Because the chiefs trusted him, they came to his cavalry camp unarmed. Miles's word was good. If he promised safe conduct, the Indians knew he meant them no harm.

White men, the chiefs told Miles, had cheated them so shamefully that they had been forced to flee their agency and threaten to ravage the countryside just to live. They had been given old, rotten beef by the contractor who supplied them. Poor flour had been given to them; they could not make bread with it. Worn-out oxen had been sold to them at top prices for their farm work. The result was that their people were starving. They could not eat what had been provided for them, and they had no fit animals to help raise food. They faced a winter in which many of their people would die unless government help came fast.

Miles's blue eyes frosted like the ice on a glacier as he heard their pitiful story with increasing anger. It was the same old story—greedy contractors and indifferent or timid Indian agents cheating the Indians and indirectly forcing them to go on the warpath. It was the same situation against which he had protested so vigorously back in Indian Territory. If he had his way he would have horse-whipped both the contractors and the Indian agents.

Quickly, for the chiefs' stories were easy to check, Miles assured himself that the Indian leaders had spoken the truth. A few greedy men were endangering the whole frontier. By forcing the Jacarillas and the Muaches to choose between peace and war, these scoundrels risked the lives of every man, woman, and child seeking to build a new land in the Southwest.

There had been attempts by others to make certain the Indians would be treated fairly, but the general realized that this time someone must be held strictly accountable. He named one of his own officers to head the agency. In this way he could keep in personal touch with dealings with the two tribes.

Then he sent off a report to Washington in which he strongly recommended that only an army officer of known integrity ever should be placed in charge of Indians; that half of the government money provided for support of the Indians on their reservations should be invested in cattle and horses for their farm use; and that Indian children should be educated in government schools. He believed they should be taught the ways of the white man so they would know how to provide for themselves without having to resort to violence. He hoped, within one generation, to change the natives from a nomadic to a pastoral civilization.

His recommendations were put into effect, but they could prove successful, Miles knew, only after the natives had been made to try out his new system.

Again, in the spring of 1876, Miles went to Colorado and Nebraska to restore peace and order. He found out what troubled the Indians, then tactfully suggested a settlement acceptable to them. Another Indian war was averted.

But Miles's diplomatic skill was not used to prevent the tragic events which soon were to take place. Perhaps had he been sent to command the Department of the Platte, as he had wished, things would have been different, but he was tied down to routine desk work at Fort Leavenworth while a major tragedy of the Indian frontier was moving onto the stage in the wild, beautiful country to the north.

FOUR

SITTING BULL AND CRAZY HORSE

The fierce Sioux Indians, the "cutthroats," had migrated westward from the region beyond the Great Lakes after the turn of the nineteenth century. They had driven before them the Crow Indians, a group of tribes almost always friendly to the white man.

The Sioux called themselves the Dakota Nation, but they were not truly a nation, since they were made up of Uncapapas, Oglalas, Minneconjoux, San Arcs, and Brules and were affiliated with the Cheyennes, Yanktonais, Tetons, Santees, and Assiniboins. The Sioux claimed the land now embraced by the Dakotas, northern Nebraska, eastern Wyoming, and eastern Montana.

93

In 1869 the Federal government gave the Sioux two reservations and promised that no whites would be permitted in the area. But, as had happened so often before, hunters, trappers, miners, settlers, railroad surveyors, and workmen soon crowded upon the Indians' land.

General Custer, Yellow Hair, whose long tawny locks were worn to the shoulder even in battle, had commanded at Fort Lincoln in the Dakota territory for some time. It was Custer who indirectly and unintentionally started the Indians on the warpath. He had publicized news of a gold strike in the Black Hills of the Dakotas. The news brought thousands of prospectors into the land where the Sioux had been peacefully hunting.

The Sioux protested that the game was being driven away. When their pleas went unheeded, they responded, as they always had, by breaking out of their reservations and taking to the warpath and the pursuit of the buffalo, their only source of food, clothing, shelter, and fuel.

There were great chiefs among the Dakota tribes. Sitting Bull of the Uncapapas was the leader. He was the fiercest of all. He hated the white man with cold, bold cunning, determined on revenge. Spotted Tail, a man of strong character, had many of the qualities of a true statesman. Red Cloud had been a great warrior and a killer of many white men, but now he was found on the conservative side in the war councils of the Dakotas. He was cautious, if not openly tired of war.

It was Sitting Bull to whom Miles later referred as the "incarnation of ferocity." Indeed, the chief of the Uncapapas was not only the most ferocious leader, but also the greatest field general among the Plains tribes. Sitting Bull was past fifty at the time of the Black Hills gold strike, but agile despite a slight limp, the result of an old battle wound. He was a compact, sturdy Indian who had been a mighty warrior in his younger days. His role now was that of the strategist who directed his people's battles, whether in fighting for their reservations or in combat.

Sitting Bull wore his hair parted in the middle and sweeping over his ears, the long ends brought forward over his chest. He had a wide, high forehead and a big nose. His tight mouth was almost always set in a grim line. The chief's eyes, his mouth, his speech, his whole manner showed the fierce, never-ending hatred which burned him as with a consuming fire. He was dedicated to but one purpose in life: driving the white man from his land. Failing that, he was determined to exact as high a price as he could as white civilization drove his people after the retreating buffalo herds.

Crazy Horse, twenty-six, leader of the Dakotas' fighting forces, was a much lighter-skinned Indian than Sitting Bull. He, too, hated white men, but not with the relentless zeal of the older chief. They were enemies, and they must be defeated in battle; and, as enemies, no torture or humiliation of their bodies was too horrible for him to carry out.

Sitting Bull had organized his people's escape from the reservations with skill and secrecy. The new outbreak of killing, burning, and looting when the Dakotas fled their reservations came so suddenly that the whole northern frontier was aflame before the Army had time to move.

But move the Army did, in the spring of 1876, determined to round up or exterminate the thousands of well-mounted, well-armed warriors who were laying waste the land in an area that would one day include five states.

The hostiles were known to be holed up somewhere in the Big Horn River country of Montana. Three army columns marched against the Sioux led by Sitting Bull and Crazy Horse. In command of the column from the south was General George Crook, the Gray Wolf, a hard-bitten old Indian fighter with many years of experience. In overall command of the joint expedition was General Alfred H. Terry, a capable general, but lacking experience in fighting Indians. He would move from the east. General John Gibbon would ride in from the west.

General Terry had sent word to Sitting Bull, Crazy Horse, and the other chiefs of the Sioux that they must be back on their reservations by January 1, 1876, or he would "come and get them." The chiefs ignored the warning and camped during the winter of 1875-1876 in the Big Horn Mountain range. There they found food for their stock and enough hunting to keep their people alive.

Sitting Bull was sure that Terry would not come for him during the most severe winter in many years in a land which usually had hard winters. The temperature was more than forty degrees below zero at times; the rivers froze, and the mountain passes were blocked by snow. The Big Horn can be a most forbidding land, however great its beauty.

True to Sitting Bull's prediction at the war council which decided not to return to the reservations, there was no activity by the Army until spring. Terry thought it impossible to go after Indians in winter. True, Custer had fought in the field during part of the winter of 1869 in Oklahoma, and Crook liked to think he was a winter campaigner, but neither of the generals had made a serious business of facing winter blasts and snow. And the hostiles knew it. The Army, like the Indians, preferred to hole up for the winter and keep its feet warm.

Crazy Horse defeated Crook's cavalry force on the Rosebud River, a tributary of the Yellowstone, on June 17, 1876. The Indians were wild with excitement and confidence. The bluecoats and the old Gray Wolf, who rode into battle with his long hair braided and tied across his chest, had been at war with them off and on for years. Surely, having defeated him in a pitched battle, they could fight any number of white soldiers that might be sent against them, especially, Crazy Horse told them, since most of his warriors had new repeating rifles and knew how to use them to good advantage. At last, Crazy Horse declared, there was a chance to settle old scores—perhaps even to drive the soldiers out of the Indians' own hunting and grazing grounds.

General Terry, setting forth on his end of the expedition, was troubled. It was apparent to him, little versed though he was in Indian fighting, that the spring and summer campaigns would be much harder and longer than he had imagined. He needed someone with a great deal of experience on the frontier and in the tactics of Indian fighting to lead his column. He gave command of the advance guard to General Custer of the Seventh Cavalry.

Custer was to operate against Sitting Bull and Crazy Horse with almost complete power to decide what he should do and how he should do it, but Terry urged him to be careful. He was not to engage any band of Indians, large or small, if he could help it. He was to wait, if he found them, for the three main cavalry columns to converge. It was known that the Indians outnumbered the troops. By combining forces there would be a better chance to round them up. And, if it came to a pitched battle, the soldiers would stand a much better chance if they fought together.

Custer, however, had never been a patient man, and more than at any other moment in his life, he thirsted for personal glory. He was in disfavor with President Grant for his testimony against Secretary of War W. W. Belknap, who was being tried for fraud. Grant resented Custer's statements as reflecting upon his administration, but knowing Custer's record in the Civil War and his achievements on the Indian frontier, the President reluctantly agreed to permit Custer to rejoin his regiment under Terry's command. Now Custer sought a chance to redeem himself in the eyes of Grant.

Reports were brought to him by trusted scouts that a large body of Indians had been seen. Thinking them to be only an advance party of Sitting Bull's main force, Custer split his command into three columns, the better to scout over a wider area more quickly. Division of his troops left Custer himself with only 262 officers and men, but he had boasted many times that the Seventh Cavalry could whip any number of Indians in a single engagement.

What Custer, so supremely confident of himself and his men, did not take enough into account was that Crazy Horse now had repeating rifles. They had been supplied to the Indians by unscrupulous traders. Custer may not have known that his formidable opponent—already rated by Miles as the best cavalryman on the American continent— had trained his braves to respond to some semblance of discipline.

Upon discovering Custer's splitting of his command, Sitting Bull and Crazy Horse quickly decided on a bold surprise move. Their tactics were simple. Crazy Horse, using almost his entire force, would cut off the three detachments one by one and wipe them out. No one was to be spared, but Sitting Bull gave strict orders that the body of Yellow Hair was not to be mutilated. Crazy Horse agreed; he respected Custer as a soldier. The Indians, outnumbering the white soldiers many times over, should have no difficulty achieving their purpose, especially since they could get within effective range with their repeating rifles.

On the banks of the Little Big Horn, Custer met what he supposed was Sitting Bull's scouting party on June 25, 1876. He decided that his 262 officers and men could drive the natives back or capture them. It would be a big victory, and Custer needed one just then. Yellow Hair gave the order and his bugler sounded the charge. The men of the Seventh went to it with saber, pistol, and carbine, following Custer's flowing mane into battle.

Within minutes Custer learned his mistake, but it was too late. He had plunged headlong into nearly all of Sitting Bull's 6000 warriors.

Crazy Horse and thousands of warriors were circling the little command with a deadly rifle fire. The Indians fired while at full gallop and took a heavy toll of Custer's men. Soon Custer, caught in the open with no shelter, was forced to dismount his men and fight from behind the bodies of fallen horses.

It was all over quickly. Not one member of the command was left alive. Custer's wounded horse, Comanche, was the only survivor. Custer's body was left intact, but those of the other troopers were horribly mutilated and stripped of their clothing, arms, and ammunition.

Major Marcus A. Reno, leading a column of the Seventh, was meanwhile under heavy attack on a hill some twenty minutes' ride away. He fought a hard daylong action. Sitting Bull kept him pinned down so that he could not go to the relief of Custer.

Captain Frederick W. Benteen, who had heard the firing on both sides of his command, delayed for precious minutes, then went to Reno's aid. The two commands finally drove off the Indians, then went looking for Custer. They found the remains of the horrible massacre. It was one of the worst defeats United States troops ever had received at the hands of Indians.

News of the disaster and the brutal slaying of his friend reached Nelson Miles at Fort Leavenworth on July 5.

Mary Miles had never seen her husband so stricken. When he told her the news, it was worse than she had expected. She knew how deep the attachment between the two men had been. Indeed, she felt as keenly for Libbie.

In the midst of grief, Miles's mind was already at work on the military problem. Again he was a soldier, intent upon the immediate task. He sank into a chair and after a minute drew out a sheet of paper. He wrote rapidly, then called an orderly. "Get this telegram off to General Sheridan in Chicago at once. And wait at the telegraph office for a reply. It shouldn't be long coming. You may read it on the way. It concerns you, too."

When the reply came, it was an order for the Fifth Infantry to entrain at once and proceed to Fort Buford, at the junction of the Missouri and Yellowstone Rivers in Montana. There the command would report to General Terry.

"When do you leave?" Mary asked when Miles showed her the tersely worded wire from Sheridan.

"We can have our special train loaded by tomorrow morning if we work all night. I have already started preparations. The train will take us as far as Yankton, South Dakota. From there it is a long ride by steamboat up the Missouri, but that is the quickest route."

"And perilous, too, of course."

Miles nodded. "Of course. Parts of the river are very treacherous. There is always danger of shipwreck. There may be Indians, but not likely. But who knows where they are now?"

There was time for no more than a hurried farewell next morning. Then Nelson Miles was gone on one of the longest, most brilliant, and most dangerous exploits of an adventurous life.

When Miles reached Fort Buford he found conditions that appalled him. It was very different from the scene he had envisioned on the long and dangerous steamboat ride from Fort Leavenworth. The fort was jammed with soldiers, Indian scouts, canvas-topped supply wagons, artillery, mules, horses, and captured Indian ponies. There were huge piles of food, animal feed, and ammunition. The Sioux were mounted on fast ponies when they rode into battle; they were accustomed to long marches with little food and water. White soldiers would have to be well-equipped to fight them successfully, but supplies and men were scrambled in complete confusion. Miles soon realized that he should have known better than to expect too much, but for a while he was as disheartened as a man of his strong convictions and great energy could be.

General Terry was an old friend. But Miles quickly learned that Terry knew almost as little about Indian fighting as he had when he had given Custer a free hand before the massacre.

"The truth is," Miles wrote to Mary from Fort Buford, "there is not a man here who has studied this question close enough or paid enough attention to his profession to conduct an Indian campaign." He was equally outspoken about the jumbled condition of the camp, and of course such remarks were resented, particularly by the officers at whom they were aimed. Crook came in for some of Miles's most caustic criticism, since it was generally assumed that Crook would have a big part in the pursuit of Sitting Bull and Crazy Horse in spite of his defeat on the Rosebud before the Custer battle. Most officers, whether they agreed or not, held their tongues. Crook was known to be a close friend of Rutherford B. Hayes, a Civil War veteran who was likely to be the next President of the United States. But not Miles! Criticizing officers, even superiors, if he thought they were in the wrong was a characteristic he never overcame. Even Terry, his old friend, was irked.

Miles had set out for Fort Buford determined to give his experience and ability to those who were preparing to avenge the Custer massacre and bring Sitting Bull and Crazy Horse in for punishment. There was only one way to do it, as he saw it. He would pursue the Indians with relentless energy, giving them no time to regroup their forces after defeat, forcing them to one position after another with no time to hunt food and, indeed, no time even to sleep. He had proved in the New Mexico and Texas winter campaign that these tactics would pay off.

Miles pleaded with Terry to let him lead a column against Sitting Bull and Crazy Horse. But Terry was cautious. He thought command of the new expeditions should go to officers who were senior to Miles. Friendship, enthusiasm, or even ability, should have little to do with his decision.

Miles fumed and fretted and was sometimes outspokenly

critical of details of plans for the expedition. He could see that the whole plan to capture Sitting Bull and Crazy Horse and compel them to return to their reservations was stalled. No one seemed to know just what to do.

The whole area of the Dakotas and Montana was in an acute state of terror. Farmers, miners, railroad men, were fearful of a wholesale Indian massacre. And with good reason, Miles thought, for Sitting Bull and Crazy Horse were raiding almost unchecked over a wide territory.

Scarcely anyone dared go anywhere without a strong military escort. Soldiers who should have been organizing as units for a march against the Indian chiefs were busy guarding wagons and protecting roads in small detachments.

Miles continued to chafe at the weeks of delay. Some of the commanders were men with little experience in fighting Indians. Others had been defeated by the savages, some more than once, and they were openly fearful that it might happen again. A defeat could ruin their military careers. Many doubtless feared they might suffer the same fate as Custer. A command surrounded by Sitting Bull and his thousands of well-trained, fast-moving warriors could be cut off and wiped out. Weeks might pass before the world would know what had happened.

Nelson Miles was anxious to get into the field and push the pursuit. He pestered General Philip Sheridan, commanding the department from Chicago, or General Sherman in Washington by letter and telegram demanding that he be given a field command. At last Sheridan telegraphed specific orders that Miles was to take his Fifth Infantry out on patrol. He was instructed, along with the commanders of other patrols, to prevent Sitting Bull and Crazy Horse from crossing the Yellowstone River and possibly escaping into Canada.

Miles had two grains of comfort in all the confusion and frustration: he had two top chief scouts on his patrol of the Yellowstone. Most renowned was thirty-two-year-old Colonel William F. Cody, even then known as Buffalo Bill. Cody, who was called Will by his friends, was a native of Iowa, but his family had settled twenty miles from Fort Leavenworth in Kansas when he was only six years old. He had hunted buffalo and other game to supply meat for the Union Pacific Railroad construction crews, and his knowledge of Indians and their ways was known throughout the West. He had been Sheridan's chief scout in 1868.

Younger by several years was Luther S. "Yellowstone" Kelly. Some said he was an even more able scout than Cody. A native of New York state, well-educated and highly intelligent, he had made several dangerous journeys alone through Indian country and had come off the victor in several fights with the savages. Kelly was as well able to defend himself as any Sioux or Cheyenne in rough-and-tumble Indian-style fighting. He had come to the frontier because he loved nature, and of all places he liked the Yellowstone country best. He knew almost every foot of it.

One day, after weeks on patrol in the early fall of that bleak country, Cody reported that he had information

Sitting Bull had escaped north across the Yellowstone. Miles was furious, but he was relieved when the scout assured him that the band had not crossed at any of the fords the Fifth Infantry was guarding.

Miles ordered a courier sent to General Terry at Fort Buford, then he swiftly analyzed the situation. It was evident to him that Sitting Bull and Crazy Horse had split up to go into winter camp. Sitting Bull and his warriors were believed to be in the vicinity of Big Dry Creek northeast of the scene of the Custer massacre. Crazy Horse had retreated to the headwaters of the Tongue and Rosebud Rivers to the southwest. There would be good hunting north of the Yellowstone and enough buffalo and other big game for Crazy Horse south of the river. The two chiefs and their bands would be only about a hundred miles apart and in constant communication by runner. They would have no trouble joining forces when it was spring and time to renew the war.

Many weeks after the chiefs separated, General Terry finally offered the command of an expedition against Sitting Bull and Crazy Horse to Miles. The new commander outlined his plan to keep his army in the field all winter, to give the Indians no rest from one day to another. He asked General Terry to authorize equipping the troops with the warmest clothes available.

Terry was skeptical. He doubted, he said, that such a plan would work. The command might freeze to death. It was much too risky.

Miles pointed out that his soldiers were toughened by wintering in Texas and New Mexico, and that if they were properly dressed, they could certainly stand any conditions the Indians could. At last Terry gave reluctant approval; it was Miles's campaign to organize, and he had been proved right too many times to doubt him now.

The Fifth Infantry and the cavalry and artillery units attached to Miles's command were outfitted in strange winter uniforms. Some of the men looked more like Eskimos than soldiers of the United States Army. Miles would lead them in his bearskin-lined greatcoat and bearskin cap with flaps that could be pulled down over his ears.

Before Miles could undertake a winter campaign, he had to have a strong cantonment to house his men, animals, and supplies between expeditions. He felt that he had not been given enough men or equipment, and said so, angering both Terry and Sheridan, but, as always, he would make do with what he had.

He built his little cantonment at the junction of the Tongue River and the broad, rolling Yellowstone. Later he built Fort Keogh a half mile away and named it in honor of Captain Myles Keogh, a popular cavalryman who had died with Custer at the Little Big Horn. The winter camp, meanwhile, would be strong enough to hold off anything less than a massive Indian attack, particularly since the expedition carried along two pieces of field artillery and plenty of ammunition. The site was so close to the river that even an Indian siege could not cut off its water supply.

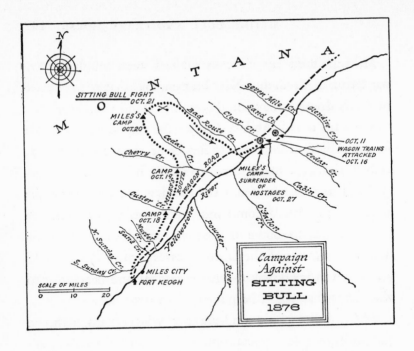

The cantonment was built of logs sunk in the ground in an upright position. The cracks between were chinked with mud. Poles were used as roofing for the huts with smaller saplings closing the holes between branches.

There were fine stands of pine on the high ground just outside the cantonment and cottonwood by the river, so there was plenty of rough-hewn timber for officers' quarters, barracks, and stables for horses and mules. The animals, too, must be protected against the icy blasts and the snows of the Montana winter.

The country north of the Yellowstone was rough, and the men felt the bitter cold as Miles and the Fifth Infantry set out from the new cantonment on October 17 to look for a supply train from Glendive, farther east. Miles suspected that it had been attacked by Sitting Bull.

He found the supply train. It had been attacked, but the Indians got such a hot reception that they broke off the engagement and fled.

Miles knew then that he was on Sitting Bull's trail, and he was determined to find the chief of the Uncapapas. He threw out extra flankers on the sides of the column and doubled his scouting force and the rear guard around the supply train. The Indians almost always tried to steal or stampede the horses of a military expedition or raid the wagon train. If they succeeded now in either venture, the column would be badly crippled and perhaps even forced back to the Tongue River cantonment.

Miles, true to his code, intended never to be surprised by the enemy.

The command had been on the march four days after rescuing the wagon train. One night the general had been awakened by the sound of rifle fire. Two bullets whizzed past his head and through the tent. If he had bounded off his cot, as he well might have, he probably would have been killed. A small band of Indians had tried to raid the picket line and either steal or stampede the horses, but alert sentries had challenged the Indians before the tethers could be cut and had fired on the invaders.

Miles reasoned that Sitting Bull himself was probably in the vicinity. It was good buffalo country. He could see herds of the great shaggy animals in the distance.

The general had an uneasy feeling. It was one he always had when there was impending danger. The command was in more open country now, with a low range of hills some distance away. The prairie grass was dry, but it was almost the only shelter within rifle range the Indians could take if Sitting Bull planned an ambush. The general was not particularly worried, but there was still that uneasy feeling he had come to recognize as a warning.

Scouts were far ahead of the column, which was tied down to the speed of the slow wagon train. Miles had doubled his flankers again. These guards marched at some distance to the right and left of the main body of troops. It would be difficult for an enemy to make a surprise attack from either side. The rear guard had been doubled to protect the supply wagons. The command was a long way from its base now. The vital necessities—food, water, and ammunition—must not be cut off. All in all, there seemed little danger of a surprise attack, but the commander couldn't be sure.

Miles wished that Cody were along with him on this expedition, but he had gone to New York to stage a Wild West show. Miles realized that in Yellowstone Kelly he had just as good a scout. The general always found himself at ease with Kelly.

Then the general saw a rider approaching fast from up ahead. As the man drew nearer Miles recognized Kelly. The chief scout must have important news to leave his post at the head of the column.

"Sir," said Kelly, reining his fast Indian pony to a dust-raising halt, "Sitting Bull's camp is just ahead over that rise."

"Are you sure?" asked Miles.

"Very sure, sir. I thought you might want to have a look yourself," Kelly replied.

The general's arm shot into the air, palm outward. The order was repeated down the line, and the weary soldiers came to a halt. They were glad of a rest, no matter how brief.

The general urged his horse forward, Kelly beside him. They broke into a gallop over the prairie and quickly came up with the main scouting party.

Miles scanned the low range of hills in the near distance with his field glasses. At first he could see nothing but the bleak bluffs. Nearer, the dry prairie grass waved gently in a little wind. There was a hint of snow in the air.

Then, as he looked, the skyline came alive with mounted Indian warriors. Some carried feathered lances, but most held rifles upraised in one hand as they guided their ponies.

There were warriors as far as Miles could see; the line of fighting men stretched far along the range of hills. Behind the front row others were riding up.

Several riders detached themselves from the silent line and came forward down the plain walking their ponies. "Looks like a truce party," the general observed. He handed the field glasses to Kelly.

After a moment the chief scout handed them back, his black eyes snapping with anticipation. "It is a truce party, sir, and it could be Sitting Bull himself."

Miles turned to one of the scouts. "The men are to be deployed at once for combat. No shot will be fired until I give the order. The field piece will be unlimbered, loaded, and made ready for action. And send Lieutenant Bailey forward."

Miles looked through the field glasses again. Across the brow of the hills he could see Sitting Bull's warriors against the skyline. They appeared to be heavily armed and mounted on good ponies. He knew they were among the best cavalry in the world for quick, sharp fighting. Nonetheless, if a peace talk failed, he had a surprise for them. Not even Indian cavalry could stand up against artillery. Still, this was open country; there was no protection for his men except the wagons.

Accompanied by six braves, Sitting Bull walked his pony down the hill and across the plain at a steady pace. The Indians appeared to be in no hurry, but only because they wanted to convince the white men that they were not afraid.

"Sitting Bull wants to feel out our strength and our determination," Miles observed to Kelly. "I don't think he wants to make real peace talk. He hates the white man too much. And, since the massacre on the Little Big Horn, and the defeat of General Crook by Crazy Horse, he doubtless thinks his braves are more than a match for all white soldiers. That makes him much more dangerous now. We must watch out for tricks."

Steadily the little group of Indian horsemen advanced across the prairie. Miles watched them through his glasses. He took careful note, too, of what was happening back on the hills. "Sitting Bull has deployed his braves for battle.

He is set for a charge," remarked Miles. Kelly looked, then nodded gravely in agreement.

Miles trained his glasses to the rear, assuring himself that his own men were being deployed for instant action. He could see dust to the rear of the column and knew that the field piece was being hauled into position.

A lone rider galloped up. It was Lieutenant Hobart K. Bailey. "Bailey, take five men and ride out with me to meet Sitting Bull," the general ordered the young officer. Quickly Bailey picked five enlisted men of the advance guard and the seven rode out to meet Sitting Bull.

It was Miles's first encounter with Sitting Bull, but he had read every scrap of information about him in official reports and had talked with many scouts who knew him well.

The stalwart medicine man of the Uncapapas sat his pony with an easy grace that came from long years of riding in the headlong, bareback way of the Indian warrior. Disdaining the war bonnets most chiefs affected during ceremonial parleys, Sitting Bull had decorated his hair with a single feather. It stuck up straight, as though in defiance, at the top of his head.

Miles saw a man of rugged features and high cheek bones, with a mouth set in a grim, unyielding line and somewhat drawn down at the corners. Sitting Bull's eyes were unforgettable. They were big and deep-set, and they burned with fierce hatred for all white men. The general felt a stab of sympathy for him. Sitting Bull had cause enough to hate white men. Perhaps it would be possible to reason with him now, but Miles doubted it. Still, he must try.

"Sitting Bull," Miles told the chief after they had exchanged formal greetings through an interpreter, "we have come to urge you, for the sake of peace between our peoples, to return to your agency at once."

Sitting Bull shook his head so angrily that his single feather seemed in danger of loosening from his braided hair. His mouth worked as though he were too angry to form words. Then he urged his pony forward several paces, as though to emphasize what he was about to say.

His voice was deeply guttural, but somewhat melodious despite his anger. Miles could understand why the man had such magnetism in the councils of his people. "No, Chief Bear Coat! I shall not return! The Great Spirit made me an Indian, but he did not make me an agency Indian!"

There was contempt in Sitting Bull's voice, and Miles thought to himself that Sitting Bull really believed he could conquer the white man. He was even more dangerous than Miles had thought. Although no diplomat where superiors were concerned when he considered them wrong or inefficient, Miles almost always sought to reason with the Indians. But the chiefs whom he had previously persuaded to return to their agencies were men of a different kidney from this defiant, wild-eyed savage.

"Why," demanded Sitting Bull through the interpreter, "does Bear Coat march with the winter winds? Why does he not return to his warm winter camp like other white generals? Why does he march against Sitting Bull? Sitting Bull seeks only to hunt the buffalo to feed his people."

Despite his anger and his hatred, Sitting Bull was trying now to control himself.

Miles ignored the questions. "We have come only to find you and to persuade you to return to your reservation. Surely whatever wrongs you have suffered can be righted once you have returned and stopped robbing and murdering innocent people."

Again Sitting Bull shook his head emphatically. He said, "How did Bear Coat know where to find Sitting Bull?"

Miles smiled grimly, and the interpreter translated the reply. "I knew," Miles assured the chief, "that you were on the Yellowstone, Chief Sitting Bull. I came with determination to bring you back to the agency, peacefully if possible, but forcibly if I must." Miles tried to make the statement calm and matter-of-fact, so as not to anger the chief further.

But now there came over Sitting Bull a startling change. From the adroit, cunning leader, however wild-eyed, that he had seemed only a second before, he changed into an enraged savage. He acted, Miles thought, like a wild beast, shaking his head as he spoke. He excited his pony so much that the animal looked as if it might throw him. The general wondered if the chief would hurl his steel-tipped lance at him.

While Miles and Sitting Bull talked, armed warriors rode down from the hills one by one. They took places behind and alongside their chief. Now there was a considerable number of them in addition to the six braves who had come with the chief originally.

Miles saw one of the new arrivals conceal a short-barreled rifle beneath the buffalo robe which he wore about his shoulders. It was apparent that the Indians planned to encircle the men of the truce party and kill them, as they had done on several occasions before.

The general turned sternly to Sitting Bull, who by then had regained some of his composure. Miles pointed to the warrior with the concealed rifle. "Does the great Chief Sitting Bull so greatly fear Chief Bear Coat that he seeks to kill him by stealth? Are the mighty warriors of the Dakota afraid, that they steal down from the hills, one by one, to break a truce? Send your braves back to the hills at once or our rifles shall speak rather than our tongues!"

Miles knew that his life and the lives of all in the truce party were in grave danger. He more than half expected Sitting Bull to give the signal for an attack at once. But he also knew that his stern warning had taken the chief of the Uncapapas by surprise. Sitting Bull had been enraged when he discovered that the hated white chief had known of his movement across the Yellowstone. Now Sitting Bull was threatened with dishonor if he did not keep his truce pledge. An appeal to honor and the suggestion that the chief might be afraid of the white men seemed the only way to avert trouble.

A short growl served to send all but the original six warriors trotting their ponies back to join the braves who still lined the hills.

Miles turned again to Sitting Bull, but his lips were tight and grim and his eyes were frosty blue. He, too, was near the end of his patience. He knew that he could not reason with Sitting Bull. "I shall give you until tomorrow morning to consider my offer. You alone shall decide between peace and war."

Miles abruptly wheeled his horse around and, with his small escort, walked back to his waiting troops. He withdrew his command three miles, to the corner of a heavy stand of timber near a swiftly flowing stream. The guard was doubled that night, and the men slept on their arms ready for an attack, but none came.

Sitting Bull and his lesser chiefs debated most of the night whether or not to accept Miles's offer. The younger chiefs and the braves wanted war. They had tasted victory on the Little Big Horn and on the Rosebud when they defeated Crook. Why should they meekly return to their agencies now when there was only this little band of infantrymen to force them back?

The next morning, October 22, Sitting Bull asked for another truce talk. He rode out with Bull Eagle, John Sans Arc, White Bull, Gall, Standing Bear, and Pretty Bear.

Miles met them at the same spot on the prairie. It was a beautiful day, and the general thought how much pleasanter it would be to go hunting than to fight this Indian statesman, for he was certain now what Sitting Bull's answer would be. "You still have a chance to return peaceably," Miles warned. "Otherwise, I shall have to take you back by force."

Sitting Bull gave a grunt of contempt and spat on the ground in front of Miles. He could offer no greater insult. "The Dakota have slain the great Chief Yellow Hair," shouted Sitting Bull. "If Chief Bear Coat is a mightier warrior than Yellow Hair, let him prove it!"

So Sitting Bull intended to fight. Miles was sorry, for he felt the chief was really more of a diplomat than a warrior, although he possessed great strategic and tactical ability in war. Evidently Sitting Bull believed his victory over Custer had given him the power to crush all soldiers.

Miles's relaxed manner turned cold and hard. He could be persuasive with the Indians, but the time for tact was gone. "I shall give you just fifteen minutes to change your mind. Then I'm coming after you." Miles turned his horse abruptly and walked it slowly back to his command. He half suspected they would shoot him in the back.

The warriors who again lined the hills and low bluffs suddenly burst into wild yells as Sitting Bull and his escort of chiefs moved back toward them at a slow pace.

"They outnumber us," Miles observed to Lieutenant Bailey, "but we have the advantage if we keep them at a distance. They're not as good shots as we are from afar."

The troops had been deployed in lines of skirmishers while the brief parley was taking place. There was no cover except the short prairie grass, and it did not help much. The upper parts of the men's bodies would be exposed. The Indians would have some protection if they rode far over to one side on their ponies, using their mounts as shields.

Already Miles could see warriors galloping along the edge of the open ground. Soon the reason for the maneuver became apparent: Sitting Bull had ordered the grass set afire. It was an old Indian trick. Quickly the blaze was crackling, giving off an acrid, choking smoke. The fire might give the Indians some advantage, including a kind of cover from the smoke.

Yelling and whooping warriors soon were circling the command on the open prairie. Miles gave the order for the men to form a hollow square. All faced outward to pour deadly fire into the ranks of the braves. It was the supreme test of the troops, and Miles was everywhere along the line encouraging his men. They held steady under the Indians' fire.

"Make every shot count!" Miles shouted. The order was scarcely needed, for the men knew they were fighting for their lives. If they didn't hold off Sitting Bull now, there would be a far worse massacre than that on the Little Big Horn.

Miles remembered hearing that General Terry had urged Custer to take along light artillery. But Custer had spurned the suggestion; it would slow up his column. Miles was glad he had a field piece. To save time and handling, Miles had brought his gun in a covered wagon where it was concealed from Indian eyes. Probably Sitting Bull did not know of it. It seemed time to put it into action. The gun was quickly brought up and trained so that it could fire straight into the center of the Indian formation.

Sitting Bull's warriors were taking advantage of the smoke from the burning prairie, but it worked to the advantage of the infantrymen, too. The riflemen fired at Indian shapes that rode, almost ghostlike, through the swirling smoke. The soldiers had better concealment, for they were nearer to the ground.

The battle raged for hours. It was hard, sweaty work, and Miles coughed and choked with his men. Horses were hard to control because they were so frightened by flame and smoke, but the Indian ponies did not seem to mind.

The braves circled the command many times on their fast mounts, firing wildly. After every assault Miles re-formed his hollow square, each man facing outward, protecting the wagon train plodding along in the center. Sitting Bull's warriors could not break through the square. Nor could they come closer than rifle range, for the men of the Fifth Infantry were all marksmen, and they held firm.

Slowly but surely the Sioux were being pressed back toward the low range of hills. Each time they retreated, Miles moved his column forward. Always he was ready to re-form the hollow square, and he gave the enemy no chance to capture the precious wagon train.

The situation was not quite so desperately uneven as it had at first seemed. For while the smoke gave the Indians some temporary protection, the individual soldiers did not present very good targets. Their high-powered rifles and deadly aim kept the savages at a considerable distance, and when the field piece opened up, Sitting Bull was forced to withdraw.

Relentlessly the hollow square pressed forward. Men fired when they could see Indians to shoot at. As the hostiles retreated out of range, the field piece was rushed forward to spread another hail of shot. The Indians were as much terrified by the loud boom of the gun as by the effect of the metal fragments it fired.

Soon Sitting Bull's camp itself was overrun and burned. Miles chased the chief down Bad Route Creek. Still Sitting Bull retreated, sometimes re-forming his warriors to make another circling charge or to make another stand behind rocks. As the day wore on, he seldom took the offensive. It was too costly in lives.

Night came and the engagement was broken off. Miles pitched camp in a valley with his wagons circled and the picket lines under heavy guard. The Indians made the night hours hideous with their yelling and dancing around a roaring council fire. Every man of the Fifth Infantry slept on his arms. Sentries drove off repeated attempts to raid the picket line.

Day dawned and the Indians were surprised when the attack was renewed. They were not accustomed to such tactics. Miles pursued them relentlessly. He chased them for two days, giving them no chance to regroup, to rest, or even to eat. Indeed, there was little food for the warriors anyway after their camp was burned. And they had no time to hunt.

For forty-two miles the Indians were chased. Then, on the banks of the Yellowstone, the general saw the band on the opposite shore and sent over a flag of truce and a demand for immediate surrender.

Even the wide river was no protection for the Sioux now. They might have held up the infantry at the ford with rifle fire from the opposite bank, but Miles had the field piece in position, and they had no stomach for more fighting against cannon.

Chief Bear Coat, they had discovered, was a different kind of soldier from the ones they had known. He could not be tricked; he could not be trapped; and they knew now that he had meant every word he said to Sitting Bull. It was better, the chiefs decided, to surrender and return to the reservation, at least until spring. They overruled Sitting Bull and sent a delegation over the river to accept Miles's surrender terms.

But not Sitting Bull. With Pretty Bear and Gall and some forty lodges he fled northward during the night.

Some of Miles's scouts thought Sitting Bull was headed for Canada, but the general did not think so. He believed the medicine man would hide somewhere north of the Yellowstone until spring, then call his people out of the reservation and join forces with Crazy Horse for more raiding and killing.

Miles was satisfied with the campaign so far. He had forced the surrender of most of Sitting Bull's band, although the chief himself had escaped, and he had shown the Indians a more determined kind of warfare than they had ever known. Because they needed to hunt buffalo or other big game and had to have forage for their ponies, they could not move camp far in winter. If he kept them on the move, they had no recourse but surrender.

If Miles was right about Sitting Bull's plans for the spring, it was vital that Crazy Horse be captured and his band split up as soon as possible. As soon as he arrived back with his regiment at his cantonment by the Tongue, Miles began making plans for a quick and decisive campaign against Crazy Horse.

Believing as he did that Crazy Horse was the most dangerous Indian opponent that the American Army was likely to encounter, Miles had once told Custer, "If you think you can ride herd over a lot of frightened Indians as you did in 1868, you are badly mistaken. Now you have Crazy Horse to reckon with." Miles recalled the conversation as he pushed plans for the new and secret expedition. It would be the most hazardous exploit of his military career to date. If he found Crazy Horse where he expected to find him—at the headwaters of the Tongue River—he estimated that the command would be some 400 miles from the nearest Northern Pacific railhead and 300 miles over impassable, snow-covered mountains to the west from the nearest settlement. Defeat under such circumstances would mean certain death for all the men of the command.

The night before the expedition was ready to set out, Miles called officers and men together at a council of war around a roaring fire on the little parade ground in the center of the cantonment. "What you men have to remember," he told them, "is that the Indian is a most dangerous warrior at 200 yards. That is the range within which he is accustomed to kill game with bow and arrow. Beyond that, where he has to estimate distance, arrange the sight of his rifle, and make allowance for the effect of wind on the flight of the projectile, he is vastly inferior to the intelligent, trained rifleman."

There was an audible expression of agreement. Some of the officers and all of the scouts already knew the fact, and many of the men, veterans of other Indian campaigns, were generally aware of it. Nonetheless, it was reassuring, somehow, to have the fact put into clear words.

"There is no such thing," Miles went on, "as order, positive authority, or discipline among the Indians in combat." The lack of organization, he added, was most important when the going got really rough. Disciplined, obedient troops had many times the chance to win over undisciplined fighters, no matter how cunning or brave. The general continued, "You will, at all times and without exception, keep the hostiles at a distance. And keep them losing. They are brave up to a point, but they cannot stand defeat. And always we shall keep on the offensive, even when we can no more than keep awake ourselves. That will keep them discouraged and dispersed."

There was silence as the general finished. "That's all. We move up the valley of the Tongue at dawn."

Only six days after Miles's arrival back at the cantonment, the expedition against Crazy Horse set off on the cold morning of December 1, 1876. The 500 men were an unmilitary-looking lot as they slogged through foot-deep snow and over frozen streams. Military spit and polish had given way to comfort and efficiency. They were dressed in wool and fur to protect them from biting winds and freezing snow. They wore wool caps with flaps to keep their ears from freezing, and they had lined their boots with heavy wool cloth to keep their feet warmer.

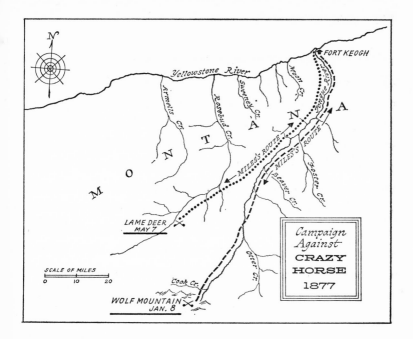

For the wintry trek over rough country the men had
been told to leave behind everything that was not absolutely essential. The men would have little use for in-fight-
ing weapons except knives and pistols. What they required
was a good rifle, plenty of ammunition, warm clothing,
enough to eat and drink to keep up strength, and enough
firewood and blankets to keep reasonably warm at night.
Much of the time they would be forced to sleep almost in
the open, sometimes on the snow. They would be lucky
when they could keep tents over their heads in the fierce
winds that blew off the mountains.

The column headed in the general direction of the foothills of the timbered Big Horn Mountains in what is now
Wyoming and Montana. Eagles screamed shrill defiance in
their flight to the peaks above as Yellowstone Kelly and the

scouts broke trail through the snow some distance ahead of the column. Now and then there came the fierce call of a mountain lion. Ice broke in the river with a loud boom, sounding like distant thunder or the roll of heavy gunfire. There came the steady crunch of packed snow being tramped into squeaky powder. Lumbering at the rear came the heavily laden supply wagons, their coverings whipped by the wind and frequently torn loose.

The mules didn't like the cold or the snow, but like good soldiers, they plodded ahead, accustomed to all kinds of weather. The horses made less fuss.

Concealed beneath the wagon bows and canvas of two of the vehicles of the supply train were field pieces. It was easier to carry them on wagons than on their high-wheeled carriages in such rough country. Besides, the guns were out of sight of Indian scouts. To all appearances, the column consisted only of winter-clad soldiers, who didn't look much like soldiers, armed only with rifles.

Miles had hoped to take Crazy Horse by surprise, but soon Kelly told him he had failed in this. There were plenty of Indian signs about, but for the moment the savages chose to remain in hiding.

For days the command scuffed through snow, the men cold despite their wool and furs. They were hungry every day long before chow time. Each evening the men scraped snow from the ground, pitched their tents, built small cook fires, prepared their meager supper, and rolled up in their blankets early to keep warm. They always slept fit-fully, expecting at any minute to hear the fierce Sioux war cry. Every man slept on his arms, ready for instant action. Fortunately there was plenty of dry wood to be had for the gathering, and plenty of water was available from melted snow.

The guards were doubled and teams of scouts were posted well out on the flanks of the encampment. Miles was living up to his first rule: Never be surprised by the enemy.

One day Kelly reported that Crazy Horse was camped just ahead, on the Tongue. The camp stretched for three miles along the frozen river.

Miles sent strong detachments after the Indians. There were several sharp skirmishes, but Crazy Horse managed to slip away. He fled with all but a few old squaws and several children into the foothills of the Wolf Mountains. He had to abandon some of his camp supplies in his flight, but for the most part he left only smoldering fires and refuse.

The mountains were rough country, far worse than the terrain over which the column had been marching. There was plenty of cover behind rocks, cottonwood and pine trees, bushes, and in ravines. Crazy Horse knew the land well since it was one of his favorite hunting grounds.

On the evening of January 7, Miles's command took up a strong position in the mountains. There was timber, water, and sufficient open land to prevent the Indians from making a surprise attack in the night.

Before sunset Indians were seen on the craggy cliffs above the camp. Yellowstone Kelly was sent up to scout the area. The mission nearly cost him his life, for the Sioux jumped his small party. They barely were rescued by Miles's quick move in sending out troops when he heard firing along the ridge.

The general had been certain after the first few miles that Indians were watching the column from a safe distance. At intervals savages were seen. Miles had been worried that Crazy Horse might attempt an ambush. Now he felt that he would meet Crazy Horse the next day, for the chief had been driven as far as he could go into the foothills. Higher up there would be no forage for his ponies and no food for the warriors, his squaws, and children. Crazy Horse must stand and fight now or surrender, and Miles did not believe that he would give up without a battle.

The general faced his officers around the campfire that evening. "Gentlemen," said Miles, "Crazy Horse is camped near us, at the head of the valley. He is doubtless expecting to catch us napping early in the morning and wipe us out as he did Custer."

There were sober nods of agreement. The command was outnumbered several times over by the Sioux.

"Crazy Horse will attack just before daylight or as the day is breaking. I want every man of this command to eat a light breakfast of hardtack and dried meat. There are to be no fires built after midnight. There will be no lights at all in camp tonight. Keep your horses as quiet as possible when you saddle up in the morning, and leave anything you don't absolutely need. Crazy Horse and his warriors will be stripped down to essentials. We shall travel as lightly as they. We shall deploy into position one hour before daylight. They won't be expecting us to move so early. Good night and get what rest you can."

Twice during the night the shots of sentries awoke the general. Skulking Indians had been chased off. Some of the savages tried, without success, to approach the tent where the captive women and children were housed. Stealthy shadows stole along the picket line and close to the supply wagons. The completely darkened camp evidently puzzled the Sioux.

Miles's horse was saddled and bridled long before daylight. With an orderly and a bugler at his side he rode out to a high bluff overlooking the Tongue valley. The light of a gray dawn slowly sharpened distant objects into focus as Miles swept the valley and the craggy bluffs with his field glasses. Crazy Horse would expect him to march up through the ever-narrowing valley. It would be a wonderful spot for an ambush or for a frontal charge by Indian cavalry.

Miles made certain that his command was deployed to the best advantage. He nodded with satisfaction as he noted that the two field pieces were already set for quick firing. His officers were doing a splendid job. If the Indians attacked they would get a hot surprise.

Light snow was falling and Miles thought there would be a hard storm within an hour or two. Snow might make fighting more difficult, but it would hamper the Indians as much as it did his soldiers. And it would make the going more slippery for unshod Indian ponies.

Soon an awesome sight appeared. Even Miles thrilled as

he watched it, his every sense alert to the dangers it implied. From up the valley came more than a thousand well-mounted and well-armed Sioux. Most of the savages were advancing slowly along the valley, as they usually did before goading their ponies into a charge. Soon Miles saw a strong group of warriors take over a bluff to the left of the troops. It could become the key to the Indian position if the fighting became close. Miles sent his orderly to tell Majors James S. Casey and Edmund Butler and Captains Baldwin and McDonald to proceed at once around the Indian flank and secure the bluff.

Still the mounted Sioux advanced. The troops held their fire. They wanted the enemy within closer range.

The Sioux were shouting now. The moisture-laden air carried their voices clearly along the valley corridor. "This is your last breakfast, white soldiers! This is your last breakfast!" they cried. The taunt was supposed to put fear into the hearts of the soldiers. Instead there were roars of laughter and shouts of defiance from the men when the scouts interpreted the challenge.

Now Miles could see a strong body of troops leave the main force. They headed for the sandstone bluff held by the band of Sioux warriors who had scaled it not long before.

As the soldiers approached the bluff, a lone warrior rode out in front of the Indian position on a spirited war pony. He was dressed in full regalia with a brightly feathered war bonnet that swept almost to the ground. There was more light now. Through his field glasses, Miles recognized

Big Crow, a brave but reckless chief who had long boasted that no white man's bullet could hit him.

A thunderous volley erupted as the main body of troops opened fire. Rifles cracked. The artillery roared into action; the two guns had been placed so that they could fire over the heads of the advancing soldiers. Shells burst among the Indian riders and a terrific hail of bullets from the soldiers' rifles cut down many warriors.

Crazy Horse had expected no such reception. He had planned at his war council the night before to take Miles's camp by surprise at dawn. He thought most of the command would be cut down before an effective defense could be organized. He had not been prepared for such effective use of the field pieces, either, though he had discovered before the battle that Miles had them. And he had not anticipated the assault on his flanking bluff.

Too late he realized that he had not taken the proper measure of his opponent this time. Miles had figured out in advance what Crazy Horse was likely to do, and when. One of the general's biggest assets was the ability to place himself in the position of his enemy and figure out his probable moves.

Miles swept the valley again with his field glasses. How he would like to be down there in the melee at the head of his men! But this was one time when he must remain in the background and direct the battle.

Three orderlies reported ready for instructions to be carried back to the field commanders. The snow was falling more heavily all the time. Soon Miles would not be able to see the action at all. The fight was getting hotter by the minute. Bullets whizzed past him as Indian sharpshooters saw the fur-coated figure silhouetted against the skyline.

Fighting was general now. Indians completely surrounded the troops, but the men held steady. They were deployed so that they could meet an attack from any quarter. They were keeping the Sioux horsemen at such a distance as to give them the advantage in handling their weapons. Just as Miles had told them, the Indian was most dangerous within bow and arrow range.

The Indians needed encouragement, something that would give them heart as they charged into withering fire. Chief Big Crow, sensing that the warriors might falter, dismounted and began a wild, defiant war dance as Major Casey's men charged. Miles just could make out the grotesque figure with the long war bonnet as he whirled and spun and stomped. The general had to admire Big Crow's bravery in the face of such intensive rifle fire. Perhaps, indeed, as he had boasted for so long, no white man's bullet could hit him.

Then Chief Big Crow leaped high into the air, clutching his breast. His rifle clattered to the stones. One bullet had killed him instantly. At the sight of Big Crow's fall the Sioux line wavered. Soon, despite the excited orders and the loud curses of Crazy Horse, the warriors, almost as one, wheeled their ponies and raced back up the valley from where they had come. The last of the Indian defenders of the flanking bluff scrambled down the steep, craggy sides and joined Crazy Horse in his pell-mell stampede for the mountains.

The field guns had been moved forward so that their range was now well advanced. For a few minutes the fleeing savages were subjected to more bursting shell fragments. The fire took a further toll before the horsemen finally vanished up the trail.

Usually Miles pursued a beaten foe, but this was one time it was more prudent to withdraw. In such weather Crazy Horse would have an excellent chance to ambush the command. The savages were hemmed in now, and they had been badly beaten. The valley was strewn with their dead, but they had managed to carry away the wounded. Since they could be starved out, there was no sense in risking the lives of soldiers in going after them.

Little Big Man, courageous Hump, Two Moons, and White Deer had been Crazy Horse's lieutenants in the wild charge against the troops, the scouts reported. But it was another chief, Little Deer, who rode out under a flag of truce the next day to ask for surrender terms.

"Return to your agencies. Give up your arms and your ponies," Miles told him.

Little Deer agreed. It was only then that Miles learned that the big prize, Crazy Horse, had escaped. Perhaps the young chief had gone to join Sitting Bull somewhere north of the Yellowstone.

The Sioux under Little Deer appeared to be glad enough to return to their reservation at once, for they were now in very sad condition. They would freeze or starve if they kept to the mountain country. At the reservation they knew they would be fed, sheltered, and given fuel and warm clothing.

Miles marched his men back to the cantonment at the junction of the Tongue and the Yellowstone and decided to wait until spring to take the field again. The troops needed rest after their hard, if short, campaigns against Sitting Bull and Crazy Horse. He must get in more supplies and strengthen his camp against a possible surprise attack by Sitting Bull and Crazy Horse when the snows melted.

There remained one important band of Indians who had not been dealt with. Chief Lame Deer of the Minneconjoux Sioux had wintered on the upper branches of the Tongue River, safe in the foothills. Until he was subdued the area would not be clear of hostiles, and there always was the danger that in the spring he, too, might join Sitting Bull and Crazy Horse.

Miles moved out of the cantonment on May 8, 1877, with six troops of cavalry, two companies of the Fifth Infantry, and five companies of the 22d Infantry. Knowing that speed was essential if Lame Deer was to be caught, he mounted his own infantrymen and those of the 22d on captured Indian ponies. He had no authority to mount his infantrymen, but that didn't bother Nelson Miles. Mounting all the men in the column would speed the expedition, and results were what counted.

Spring was livening the Tongue valley with green and the color of wild flowers as the column advanced. Already grass was tall. The land was much more hospitable than it had been only a few months before, when footsore and weary infantrymen slogged through knee-deep snow.

The danger from lurking Indians was almost as great as it had been in the winter, however. True, some of the lesser chiefs who had escaped with Crazy Horse had come in with their warriors to surrender rifles and ponies. There was now a considerable Indian camp just outside the cantonment, and Miles was feeding, clothing, and sheltering the natives. Lame Deer was still loose, though, and he could be expected to fight. Miles intended to surprise the chief if he could.

Sixty miles from the cantonment the general cut loose from his wagon train, leaving one company of the 22d to guard it. The column resumed the march with only a pack train to carry supplies. The wagons would follow at a much slower pace.

The Rosebud River was in flood, as were all of the creeks and streams. Miles later wrote that its crossing was "amazingly laborious." Two days were needed for the command to get to the side of the river where the hostiles were likely to be found.

Then, on Muddy Creek, a tributary of the Rosebud, Kelly's scouts found Lame Deer's camp. The village was taken by a charge led by Major James S. Casey of the Fifth Infantry and Lieutenant Lovell H. Jerome of Troop H, Second Cavalry. The chief offered little resistance in the camp, but retreated to bluffs surrounding the village. There he put up a spirited defense, but it was not successful.

Lame Deer, Iron Stone, five hundred ponies, and fifty-one lodges were captured. The ponies were used as remounts for the infantrymen who had lost their animals in the fighting. The rest were sent back to the cantonment.

A little later Crazy Horse and almost 2000 braves came in and gave up their arms and ponies. He was killed some time later while resisting arrest at the Red Cloud agency to which Miles sent him.

With the roundup of this last band of Sioux the area south of the Yellowstone had been cleared of hostiles actively on the warpath. Miles's unorthodox tactics and relentless pursuit had cleared the vast territory of some 7000 savage warriors bent upon death and destruction to all white men. And he had done it with fewer than 500 troops! Miles had revolutionized warfare against the Indians.

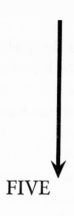

FIVE

CHIEF JOSEPH AND THE NEZ PERCES

NELSON MILES stood on the parapet of newly built Fort Keogh on the afternoon of September 17, 1877. So much had happened in the past few months. In June Mary and Cecelia had joined him. With them on the journey up the turbulent Missouri by steamer was her sister, Elizabeth Sherman. Elizabeth was still a guest in the new house Nelson had built for his wife at Fort Keogh. Miles had led a new expedition against Sitting Bull, the only result of which was to drive the chief over the border into Canada. Now Washington absolutely forbade him to cross the boundary and capture the wily Uncapapa, but the Royal Northwest Mounted Police had promised to hold Sitting Bull in check.

Miles had followed closely reports of the revolt of Chief Joseph of the Nez Perces. At first he had thought the Indians would never get as far east as his District of the Yellowstone. After all, General Howard and General Gibbon were in the field seeking the fleeing tribe. But Miles knew that Howard had been outwitted by Joseph and that Gibbon had been defeated. Now reports seemed to indicate that Chief Joseph might be heading east.

General Howard had sent word that he had lost Joseph's trail. Miles felt sure that the chief intended to join Sitting Bull in Canada. Where else could he go? What such a combination of forces would lead to was anyone's guess. Miles did not intend to wait to find out.

Miles knew Joseph only by reputation, but it was said that the handsome thirty-five-year-old chief was truly a prince among savages. Unlike most Indian leaders, he did not permit the scalping and mutilating of his victims, no matter what the provocation. He was tolerant and kind with most white men, but he was passionately devoted to his beautiful Wallowa Valley, from which land-hungry white men had forced his tribe to emigrate. Such bitterness as must now possess the chief quite probably had changed him. The Nez Perces had been at peace with the white man for more than a hundred years, but now Joseph was desperate. He had proved that he could fight and win. He might do so again.

On August 3, Miles had sent a big force of friendly Crow Indians and a troop of cavalry under Lieutenant J. C. Doane to the Judith Basin, near the Missouri River, to

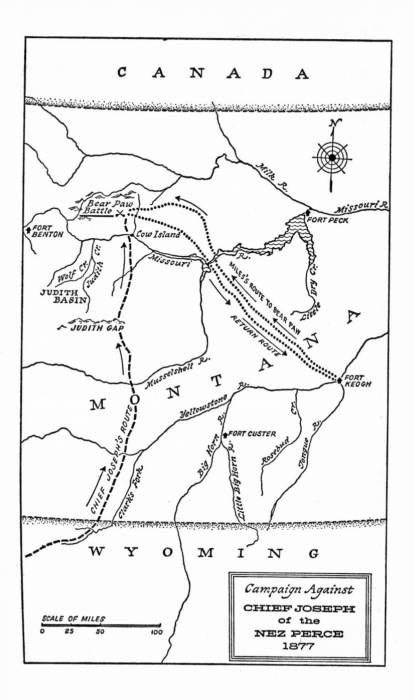

C A N A D A

Milk R.

N

Missouri R.

FORT PECK

Bear Paw Battle ✕

FORT BENTON

Cow Island

Wolf Cr. *Judith Cr.*

Missouri

JUDITH BASIN

R.

MILES'S ROUTE TO BEAR PAW

Little *Dry Cr.*

JUDITH GAP

RETURN ROUTE

N

A

FORT KEOGH

Musselshell R.

M   O   N   T   A

Yellowstone   *R.*

CHIEF JOSEPH'S ROUTE

Big Horn R.   FORT CUSTER

Rosebud *Cr.*

Tongue R.

Little Big Horn R.

Clarks Fork

W   Y   O   M   I   N   G

SCALE OF MILES
0   25   50   100

Campaign Against
CHIEF JOSEPH
of the
NEZ PERCE
1877

scout. A week later he had sent General S. D. Sturgis with six troops of the Seventh Cavalry, Custer's old command, to Judith Gap, an area much used by Indians in their north-south marches, and the upper valley of the Yellowstone to intercept the Nez Perces if they attempted to cross. Miles had not heard from Howard, Sturgis, or Doane for five weeks.

Miles was worried. Anything, he reflected, might have happened.

Suddenly he froze, all senses alert. Two objects on the bluff appeared in bold relief against the fading light. Then slowly, almost as one, they climbed down the steep trail to the water's edge. Miles took a longer look, this time through his field glasses. They were a man and a horse. The man wore a cavalry uniform. He was signaling to the fort to be taken across the river. Within minutes the cavalry-man and his mount were ferried over. He was a courier from General Sturgis.

"Have you been in a fight?" Miles asked. He could not keep deep concern from his voice. He might be about to hear of another massacre.

"No, sir," replied the courier, "but we had a good chance to have one." The man told Miles that Chief Joseph and Chief Looking Glass had eluded General Sturgis, turned his flank, and left him far behind in the chase. There was a similar report from General Howard, who had assumed command of Sturgis's force in the field. The two officers had followed the Indians' trail until it was lost in the Judith Basin. They wanted Miles to help them.

The report was five days old. It had taken the courier that long to make his way to Fort Keogh. Five days! What might have happened to Howard, Sturgis, and Doane in that time! Miles had not forgotten that Joseph had already defeated Gibbon.

"Get some food and a little rest and report to me at headquarters in an hour," Miles told the trooper. He could see that the man was almost ready to drop from fatigue, but there was work to be done, and fast. The trooper would have to get his sleep later.

Miles had been right again! Chief Joseph had swung north from the Yellowstone Park area, straight for the Judith Basin and Judith Gap. Without a doubt Joseph would cross the Missouri River and head for Bear's Paw Gap. From there he would have an easy march over the border into Canada, where Sitting Bull would be waiting for him.

Miles hoped he could block Joseph's way and then persuade him to return to a reservation. He was reputed to be a reasonable man. Miles did not blame Joseph for his action. Nonetheless, the Nez Perces must be stopped.

Within minutes orderlies were scurrying about, summoning troop and company commanders, battalion leaders, and regimental commanders to headquarters. Not the least important was the quartermaster, the officer in charge of supplies and transport.

Orders were given to equip three troops of the Second Cavalry, three troops of the Seventh Cavalry, and four companies of Miles's own Fifth Infantry. A detachment of Indian and white scouts was to be commanded by Lieutenant M. F. Maus of the First Infantry; a pack train and two pieces of artillery, including a Hotchkiss gun, an early type of machine gun, were to go along.

Rations for the men, oats for the horses, medical supplies, tentage, and ammunition were packed and stored. Messages were dispatched by courier to the commanding officers at Fort Buford and Fort Peck to send steamer supplies up the Missouri.

Officers and men worked all night. By morning the expedition had been ferried over the Yellowstone and had set off to the northwest, cavalry guidons snapping in the breeze.

Once again ignoring the rules, Miles had mounted his infantrymen on captured Indian ponies. Forced marches over the high, rolling prairie north of the Yellowstone brought the command within six miles of the Missouri on September 23. There the general sent an officer ahead to the river. If there were a steamboat in the vicinity she could ferry his men across much more safely and quickly than they could cross by any other means.

The next morning, when Miles reached the Missouri, there *was* a steamer, her tall stack belching greasy black smoke from the cordwood she was burning to keep steam in her boilers. A battalion of troops was ferried across the river on the steamboat. They would scout on the north side.

Miles believed that Chief Joseph's band was probably still in the Judith Basin, south of the river, so he set off at once on another forced march, this time westward. He hoped to surround the Nez Perces and cut them off before they could get across. The steamer cast off her moorings and started back down the river with a shrill whistle of farewell.

Some time later that day Miles and his troops met two hunters coming down the Missouri in a rowboat. They told him they had seen Indians crossing forty miles to the west, at a place known as Cow Island.

Miles's main strength was on the south bank of the Missouri. One battalion of troops was scouting the river on the north side. If they were attacked by Chief Joseph, they would be greatly outnumbered. They could hope to do no more than Custer's men had done—die with their boots on!

Time was vital. Miles had to get his whole command across the Missouri and save his lost battalion. Even more important, he had to reach Bear's Paw Gap before Chief Joseph. The wily Nez Perce chief had already led his people on the longest and most successful Indian march ever made. He had beaten one cavalry force and eluded two other commands. There seemed to be little to prevent him from carrying out his intention to meet Sitting Bull and renew the Indian wars.

Miles thought for a long moment after receiving the startling news from the hunters. Then he slapped his thigh with a gauntleted hand. "That's it! Frank Baldwin!"

Captain Baldwin had been invalided home from hard service and was sailing on the steamboat. Miles quickly dispatched his orderly to ride down the river, intercept the boat, and tell Baldwin to bring her back.

The steamer was so far downstream that Miles could not even see the black smoke from her tall stack. How was the orderly to catch up with her? How would he signal her even if he did? And would the captain put the steamboat about and come back? This was a treacherous part of the river, and such a maneuver would be highly dangerous. Something more had to be done to make absolutely certain that the boat should return.

Hardly had his orderly disappeared down the trail to the east when the general ordered another trooper to ride back and have a gun unlimbered and loaded. By the time the gun had been wheeled into position, Miles himself had galloped down to the rear. "Commence firing," he ordered the artillerymen, "and keep it up at intervals until I tell you to stop. Captain Baldwin is one of the most astute officers of this command. When he hears the sound of cannon fire, he will know it is a distress signal. If I know him, he will order that steamer put about and she'll be here shortly. Then we'll get over the Missouri quickly without getting our feet wet."

The gun boomed. The sound of the explosion, Miles knew, could be heard for many miles down the valley. Again the cannon spoke, the explosion echoing and re-echoing down the canyon walls. Miles waited, confident that his emergency summons would bring Baldwin.

With relief but no surprise the general saw a column of thick, black smoke billowing along the bluffs downstream some time later. Soon the steamer hove in sight around a bend. She was having a hard time, he could see, forcing her way against the strong current and evading jagged rocks. There was much clanging of the engine bell as her captain gave quick orders to meet half a dozen emergencies, any one of which could have piled the boat up on a rock along the shore.

Finally she made it. Captain Baldwin had heard the cannon and had ordered the boat put about and headed back upstream. Her skipper had protested because of the danger, but Baldwin had insisted. Troops, artillery, and wagon train were quickly ferried across the river, and the race against time and Chief Joseph was pushed harder than ever.

Miles rode at the head of the column on the morning of September 30. He seemed refreshed although he had been up half the night making plans and going over maps. He had to figure just how and where he might expect to intercept Chief Joseph and his band.

A courier had ridden in from General Howard the day before to report that he had given up the chase. The Idaho commander was returning to his base with his mounted infantry. He turned back Sturgis's Seventh Cavalry to Miles, but no one knew where Sturgis was at the moment. He probably would be no help in the fight that almost certainly lay ahead.

Miles marched his command along the base of the east slope of the range of the Little Rockies. Scouts and guides rode on the crest and along the west slope, well concealed from Indian eyes.

Somewhere probably still farther west was Chief Joseph,

but for the moment there were no Indians to be seen. Joseph was keeping his band well hidden. Miles believed that Joseph did not know there were any troops near, but he could not be sure. In the wild countryside he took elaborate precautions against surprise and ambush.

Troops on the march often shot game to supplement their rations, and it seemed that the forced march to Bear's Paw Gap was the best chance of good hunting Miles had ever seen. Thousands of deer, elk, buffalo, and even one huge bear had been seen, but not one rifle cracked. The general had not had to explain that even a single shot would give the alarm to Chief Joseph. The starting of wild animals from their feeding might be enough to arouse the suspicion of Indian scouts and cause them to investigate. Their eyes were keen, and while they might not see the troops winding along the base of the foothills, they would be sure to see birds taking to the air in fright.

The horses made relatively little noise on the march, for they were being ridden as much as possible off the cleared areas. There was no betraying creak of wagon axles, and there were no protests from overburdened mules, for the supply train had been left behind on the trail under Captain D. H. Brotherton's command. It would catch up with the main column as soon as it could. A mule packtrain would provide food, ammunition, and other supplies temporarily.

The men were in a sober mood, most of them strangely silent. There was a feeling that something must happen soon. All of them realized that at any moment they might hear the Nez Perce war cry. In a twinkling they would be fighting for their lives. Miles hoped to surprise Chief Joseph, but there was always the chance that Joseph might strike first.

A friendly Crow Indian came galloping back from far in advance of the column. "Nez Perce camp! Nez Perce camp!" he gasped. Riding forward to investigate, Miles saw that the half-circle camp was indeed just ahead. It was pitched in the far end of the valley. High bluffs blocked either end.

At the first warning, Miles had halted the column and barked sharp orders. Within seconds the command was girding for action. Men looked to carbine and rifle and ammunition belt. Troop and company commanders ordered them to check their pistols. Cavalrymen made sure their heavy sabers could be quickly drawn.

Despite the chilly weather, Sioux and Cheyenne allies quickly stripped off the old clothes and hats they wore on the march right down to their loin cloths. Bright feathered war bonnets appeared from their saddle rolls. They loosened scalping knives at their belts and strung bandoliers of ammunition across their backs and chests. Repeating rifles were grasped firmly as they dropped from their trail ponies and mules and vaulted lightly onto the fresh war ponies they had been leading. Only a rider's knees and a lariat about the neck and under the jaw were needed to guide one of these swift, highly trained animals. Quickly the Indians herded their abandoned trail mounts into a nearby ravine. There the animals would be relatively safe and could be collected after the fighting.

Captain George Tyler was ordered to swing around the

Indian camp and cut off its pony herd. If Miles could set the Indians afoot, they would have to stand and fight behind whatever kind of shelter they could find. They would not be able to make their favorite kind of attack, a circling charge of mounted warriors.

When other troop dispositions had been made, Miles ordered his bugler to sound the charge. Instantly every horse and pony was nudged to a fast trot, then to a gallop, as the extended line of troopers and mounted infantry raced across the valley toward the Indian camp. Into the camp charged the Seventh Cavalry, some of the men singing "What Shall the Harvest Be?" The mounted Fifth Infantry rode right with the Seventh.

Cavalry carbines pinged; infantry rifles cracked. The horses upset tepees and scattered cooking fires. Troopers and infantrymen yelled like demons. No charging Indians ever made a more hideous din. The Seventh was avenging Custer. The Fifth was fighting for a beloved commander.

Most of the Nez Perce warriors were in their lodges when the attack came; only a few squaws had been outside preparing the morning meal. Chief Joseph rallied his forces quickly after the first surprise charge. Warriors grabbed their rifles and poured heavy return fire into the attackers' ranks. The Indians were fighting not only for their lives, but also for their very way of life. To their ordinary courage was added the bravery of desperation as Joseph held them firm in the face of heavy fire.

Miles saw Captain Owen Hale leading his men. Then Hale was down, shot in the first volley from the rallying

Indians. Troopers were falling all too rapidly as Indian marksmen got the range.

Now the infantry rode up close to the camp on their captured ponies, dismounted, and fought on foot. They took what shelter they could find, leaving their mounts to graze contentedly with little concern for the heavy firing.

Quickly the heavy infantry fire countered that of the Indians, but soon the battle became a hand-to-hand struggle. This was one time when Miles's rule of keeping the Indians at a distance could not be applied. The village had to be taken, but he had scarcely expected such spirited resistance and quick response from Joseph's men.

Sitting his black charger on a little rise, Miles seemed once again to be proof against enemy fire. Bullets zinged around him like angry hornets, but he was not hit. He had some difficulty controlling his mount, however, for the frightened animal snorted and trembled with excitement.

Now the Nez Perces retreated under heavy fire, but their deadly rifles were at too close range to allow another frontal attack by the cavalry. The Indians were trying to pick off officers and sergeants. Shoulder straps and chevrons made excellent targets for the native marksmen.

Miles changed tactics. His bugler sounded recall. Then the general withdrew his men and dismounted the cavalry to fight on foot alongside the infantry. They took what shelter they could.

The fight settled down to one of exhaustion. The sharp crack of rifles was almost constant on both sides. Apparently Joseph was well supplied with ammunition, thanks, no doubt, to dishonest traders back in Idaho and to raids along the march eastward.

Captain Tyler rode up to report that he had surprised and driven in the Indian herders on the flank and captured about 800 of Chief Joseph's best war ponies, horses, and mules. Without animals the Nez Perces could not resume their march to Canada, even if they should escape the troops.

The savages were trapped in a big ravine. They could hold off the soldiers with rifle fire as long as their ammunition lasted, but they could not resume their flight northward. Quickly the troops were redeployed so that they completely surrounded the camp, or what was left of it.

Then the general counted his losses. It had been a costly battle. Two officers and twenty-two enlisted men had been killed. Many more were wounded, and the mule packtrain carried only a limited amount of medicines and bandages. It was bitter cold, and snow covered the ground. The wounded faced extreme hardship until Captain Brotherton could come up with the wagon train.

The firing slowed down. Chief Joseph was conserving his ammunition now that the soldiers were as well protected behind the excellent cover of rocks and boulders as his warriors.

Snow began to fall once again, and Miles could not shake off a gnawing worry that had been at the back of his mind ever since the command had set out on this expedition. What if Sitting Bull should come down to aid Chief Joseph? Were there troops enough to hold off the combined forces of the Indians? Miles dispatched a courier to General

Terry at Fort Buford asking for reinforcements, just in case. Then he sent one of his best scouts to try to locate General Sturgis's cavalry and lead the troopers to Bear's Paw Gap. They, too, might be needed before this battle was decided. Scouts were sent out to watch for the possible movement of Sitting Bull toward Bear's Paw Gap.

The uneasy night after the first day's battle passed with snow still falling. Nobody had more than a few hours of sleep.

The Nez Perces, too, were exhausted from the daylong battle. They were relatively quiet during the hours of darkness.

At dawn the wagon train under Captain Brotherton and four companies of mounted infantry rolled into the widely encircling camp to the cheers of the tired troops. Now there would be more food and the wounded could be treated properly. Tired though the new arrivals were from their long forced march, they had to take their places at once in the line. There always was danger that Chief Joseph might mass his warriors at some point and try to rush the camp. He might attempt to shoot his way out of the trap, for desperate men fight desperately.

Shortly after breakfast two days later Miles saw a group of Indians approaching from the head of the ravine into which Joseph and his tribe had fled with what they could salvage from their wrecked camp. Through his field glasses the general identified Joseph as the leader of the party. One warrior carried a white cloth on a pole as a flag of truce.

Within minutes the opposing leaders met, midway between the entrance to the ravine and the army's line of encampment. Chief Joseph's handsome face was lined with care, and his eyes seemed sad as he faced Miles. The two men exchanged a long, appraising look. They had not met before, but each knew well and favorably of the other. Miles's word was good. Joseph could be trusted.

The chief outlined his request through an interpreter. All he wanted—all he ever had wanted—was for his people to be allowed to return to their beautiful home in the Wallowa Valley in Idaho. He wanted to be free from the invasion of white settlers, miners, and railroad men. The land had been given to the Nez Perces by solemn treaty, and the treaty had been broken.

Miles felt deep sympathy for the chief who had led his people so far over the mountains. He had studied the report of the commission that had forced the Nez Perces from their home. General Howard himself had been a member of the board, but Miles did not believe that the order was either legal or fair. Nonetheless he had a job to do now, and that came first.

At his own suggestion, Chief Joseph accompanied Miles back to the army lines as a hostage and was treated with every courtesy due his rank. Miles liked the chief and Joseph seemed to have confidence in him. The big, bluff, straightforward soldier was trusted by other tribes. Joseph was convinced that he could be trusted now.

Snow was falling the next morning when a soldier of the outer guard rushed up to Miles's tent to report, "Indians! A large body of Indians is approaching the camp!"

In a moment the bugler's clear notes cut the snowy air. They sent the camp into a rush of well-ordered activity. Within minutes the troops in all stages of dress and undress had been formed by troop and company. Each man carried his rifle or carbine and ammunition ready for battle.

What could he do to shelter the wounded, Miles wondered? There were thirty who could not walk. What was he to do to guard the captured horses, ponies, and mules? He could not afford to lose them. How best was he to dispose his troops to meet the new enemy? He might be caught between two fires, even surrounded, if this new danger proved to be Sitting Bull coming to the aid of the Nez Perces. The fact that Chief Joseph was in the army camp would make no difference to Sitting Bull.

It was snowing so hard now that all the sentries could make out was a mass of dark objects descending from the hills. Before Miles could complete hurried arrangements to meet any new danger, there came a cry of a sentry, "Buffalo! Buffalo!"

The general joined in the hearty and relieved laughter. A big herd of buffalo, driven by cold and snow from the north, could be seen more clearly now, moving at a fast pace over the prairie. The "Indians" passed on by the camp without paying it the slightest attention.

As for the Sioux, Miles later learned that instead of going to the aid of the Nez Perces, Sitting Bull had broken camp and retreated forty miles farther northward. Even with the help of Chief Joseph's warriors, he had no stomach to take on Chief Bear Coat again.

Meanwhile, the general sent Lieutenant Lovell H. Jerome to scout the Indian camp. Jerome was to learn what conditions were from a safe distance, but he was an eager young man and more courageous than prudent. He ventured so close to the camp that he was captured. Then the Nez Perces, much to Joseph's disgust, sent word that they would not release Jerome until Joseph himself returned to his people. Joseph reluctantly went back to his own camp. The peace talk was interrupted for two days before new arrangements could be made.

Then Joseph once again came within the army lines and received Miles's assurance that he would do all that he could to have the Nez Perces' wishes carried out. Miles admitted that he could not guarantee results, but he would do his best to have the tribe sent back to Idaho.

Joseph handed his rifle to Miles in the presence of some of his chiefs as a symbol of surrender.

"I am tired of fighting," he said. "Our chiefs are killed. Looking Glass is dead. The old men are all dead. It is the young men who say yes or no. He who led on the young men is dead. It is cold and we have no blankets. The little children are freezing to death. My people, some of them, have run away to the hills, and have no blankets, no food; no one knows where they are—perhaps freezing to death. I want to have time to look for my children and see how many of them I can find. Hear me, my chiefs. I am tired; my heart is sick and sad. From where the sun now stands I will fight no more forever."

Miles himself was heartsick at the cost on both sides of

a task that had to be done. But after the surrender of this worthy foeman he began at once to provide what relief he could for the sorely stricken tribe of the Nez Perces—giving food, clothing, blankets, and shelter to the people. He won their instant praise and lasting affection for his humane dealing with them.

Of the 750 who had begun the trek from Idaho, 400 of Joseph's people surrendered with him. He had lost nearly half of his tribe in the effort to find peace and a new home. Some had died in battle, others of disease or old age. Many had starved on the trail.

Hump, the handsome young chief of the Oglalas Sioux who succeeded Crazy Horse, had become one of Miles's most trusted scouts. He had lived up to his reputation as a great warrior. One of a band of thirty Sioux and Cheyenne allies, Hump had dashed into the camp of the Nez Perces in the first charge and killed two men with his own hands. He had been severely wounded in the fighting. As soon as peace terms were settled, Miles made one of the gestures which had earned him the respect of his Indian allies. He told Hump and the other Indians to choose five ponies each from Chief Joseph's captured herd; then he gave the scouts permission to return at once to Fort Keogh.

There was something more than generosity in the gesture, for the general well knew that the Indians would travel much faster than his column with the wagon train, the wounded, the captured mounts, and the Indian prisoners. News of the great victory and Joseph's surrender would reach the fort on the Yellowstone much sooner, and it would ease the minds of the wives who had been left behind at the post.

General Terry gave immediate praise for Miles's quick move. Sheridan was equally high in his praise, but Sherman tempered his congratulations by sharing them with General Howard, who had pursued but lost the Indians. "Of course General Miles and his officers and men are entitled to all honor and praise," wrote General Sherman, "for their prompt, skillful, and successful work; while the others, for their long, toilsome pursuit are entitled to corresponding credit." As a result of newspaper stories, however, the public realized that it was Miles who had rounded up the Nez Perces and prevented another Indian uprising. Some thought his casualties a bit high, but the big story was that he had prevented another frontier war.

The Indians were rounded up after the battle and herded with their meager belongings into a long line, under guard. Then they were marched back to Fort Keogh. Miles intended to keep them under close guard in the nearby Indian camp, then in the spring send them back to their old reservation in the Wallowa Valley of Idaho.

Before the spring freshets roared through the mountain passes, however, settlers had persuaded Sherman not to send the Indians back to their beautiful valley or anywhere near their old hunting grounds. Instead, Miles received peremptory orders to ship the natives by steamer to Fort Leavenworth, and then to the lowlands of Indian Territory. The Nez Perces had caused too much trouble this one time. Besides, white men coveted the rich lands in the Wallowa Valley, and they had more influence in Washington.

Miles was furious. He told Sherman that he had promised Chief Joseph and the Nez Perces that he would return them to Idaho. What the Federal government now proposed to do was, in effect, break a solemn promise that had the effect of a treaty. Miles argued in vain. The greedy white settlers won; the Indians were sent to Indian Territory. In the lowlands many of the mountain people died. Miles continued his hot fight for them for a long time, winning little but abuse from jealous white men and uneasy officials for taking up the cudgels for the "hostiles." Sherman, many congressmen, and other influential citizens were greatly incensed by Miles's continued battle on behalf of the Nez Perces, and they were not quick to forget his forceful defense of the Indians' plea to live in peace. Only Chief Joseph, who remained Miles's friend for life, seemed to appreciate his efforts.

Defeat of Chief Joseph had one outstanding effect on the Indians north of the Canadian border. Some of the more important chiefs, including Rain-in-the-Face, who some said had personally killed Custer, Spotted Eagle, Broad Tail, and Kicking Bear, soon came in with their followers and surrendered to Miles. At one time during the year he had nearly 2000 Indians in the camp outside Fort Keogh.

SIX

NELSON MILES,
THE MAN ON THE SPOT

THERE was relative peace now on the frontier. True, Sitting Bull still raided near the Canadian border, but he was no immediate threat to the Yellowstone country. The general decided to take a holiday. Mary and Cecelia, with four other army wives and two children, accompanied him and members of his staff on an expedition up the banks of the Yellowstone in the autumn of 1878. Ten officers and a picked group of 100 veteran riflemen rode as escort. Miles took along his favorite hunting dogs.

It was a delightful trek toward the mountains. Plenty of equipment was aboard the wagon and packtrains. Hardly ever was the party out of sight of game. There were bear, deer, antelope, grouse, and quail. The dogs had a wonderful time hunting. The streams were high and filled with fish. Their table never lacked the best of wild foods, for all the men in the party were crack shots, and the fishing was easy even for amateur anglers.

Far up the Yellowstone, just as Miles was about to set out one day with his dogs to hunt a big stag the scouts had reported in the foothills, a courier rode in with the report that the Bannock Indians had broken out of their Idaho reservation and into Montana. It was Miles's territory, and he acted at once.

The women and children, including Mary and Cecelia, he sent under armed escort to Fort Ellis, the nearest army post. Then, with his little command, he set out to round up the Bannocks. His men would be outnumbered many times, but that made no difference.

There were two passes by which the Bannocks could come out of Yellowstone Park. Miles sent forty men under Lieutenant Bailey to Boulder Pass, 115 miles away. He sent word ahead to the friendly Crow Indians that he wanted warriors to join his small command to help him fight the Bannocks, their traditional enemies.

At the Crow agency, Miles sent for the chief. The head of the tribe looked around. He saw only thirty-five enlisted men sitting at ease in their saddles. "Where are the rest of your men?" inquired the chief.

Miles grinned, waved a hand in the direction of his troopers, and replied, "This is my entire command." He said it as though he were riding at the head of a thousand men. There was confidence in his tone and manner, but it did not satisfy the chief. He shook his head.

No inducements could persuade the Crows to join the little column of blue-clad troopers. Miles was disappointed, but still determined to round up the Bannocks. He moved on.

He did not know it, but the Crows had been greatly impressed by Bear Coat's decision to press on alone against such a big force of Bannocks. The column had not moved far before two Crow warriors came tearing after it. Reining in the ponies before Miles, one of them declared, "We are the bravest warriors in the whole Crow tribe. We are not afraid to fight the Bannocks with you!"

Miles welcomed their help and praised their courage, but he was not prepared for what happened during the next few hours. By twos and threes, then in larger groups, other Crows rode up to join the column and volunteer their help. All were dressed in war paint and feathers and armed for battle. Soon he had seventy-five Indian recruits.

The Crows were excellent scouts and knew the country well. The general sent them out in advance, on the flanks, and to the rear of the soldiers. "This looks more like an Indian war party than a column of United States troops," Miles commented with a chuckle. And so it might have seemed to one observing the column from a distance. The Crow warriors were a good screen for the troops.

When the combined troop and Indian column reached Clark's Fort Pass, scouts reported no signs of Bannocks. Miles began to wonder if he had miscalculated. If the Bannocks had escaped, widely scattered settlements over a vast area of Montana soon might be in for very serious trouble.

He holed up his command in a snug mountain pocket, where it would be concealed from enemy eyes, and bedded down for the night. No campfires and no lights of any kind were allowed. Then he tried to figure out his next move if the Bannocks failed to show up. He was almost certain he had arrived at the pass ahead of the Indians, but he could not be sure.

Early the next morning, through powerful field glasses, Miles spied the unsuspecting Bannock war party winding down the narrow mountain trail. The Indians pitched camp about five miles across the valley from where Miles's command was hidden.

All the rest of that day and during a part of the night, Miles kept his men and the Crows under cover. Then, sure that the Bannock camp was only lightly guarded, he passed troops and Indians quietly through the grazing Indian pony herd.

With wild yells from the troops and high-pitched war cries from the braves the command charged the Indian camp. The Bannocks were taken completely by surprise. There was a short, sharp hand-to-hand fight, but soon Miles realized that the troopers were doing all the fighting. There were no Crows anywhere about.

And no wonder, for the Indians who had made such big promises of helping to fight the Bannocks were busy rounding up the captured ponies! After the battle was over there wasn't a Bannock pony or a Crow warrior to be seen. The Crows had come along only for the loot.

Miles sent the captive Bannocks to Fort Custer and then

his wife and daughter and their guests rejoined the expedition up the Yellowstone.

The people of Montana were so grateful to Miles that they urged the government to promote him and establish a new department. Governor Benjamin F. Potts, speaking for the citizens, asked Sherman to put Miles in command of all troops assigned to the territory.

Sherman at last wrote sharply to Miles. In effect his letter was a reprimand. He told Miles that he could not promote him to brigadier general, because there were no vacancies. The number of general officers allowed by law was limited. He had no authority to set up a new department for Montana with Miles at its head. Again Miles had to be content with official commendation for his resourcefulness and enterprise.

Nelson and Mary Miles spent most of the winter of 1878-1879 on leave in Washington. While there, Miles had tried to get permission to go after Sitting Bull in Canada. He had been told plainly, by General Sherman among others, that he would cross the international line only at the risk of ruining his military career. The Canadian authorities would not permit American troops to cross the border in pursuit of Sitting Bull, and they were trying to be as diplomatic as possible with the Sioux. Apparently they feared that Sitting Bull might turn his attention to burning and pillaging in Canada, too.

In the spring Miles was assigned to command the newly created District of the Yellowstone. The dashing, magnetic soldier had become a legend on the frontier to all but his rivals and a few of his superiors. Some of them, with some eastern newspapers, thought Miles too rash, but their opinion was not at all shared by settlers in the new country. They regarded him as a bold leader—just the right man for the job of protecting the frontier.

When Miles returned to Fort Keogh, district headquarters, from his leave, he found that Sitting Bull was even more troublesome than usual. The chief still maintained his camp in Canada, but despite the watchful eye of the Royal Northwest Mounted Police, he managed all too often to slip over the border into the United States. A brief orgy of murdering, robbing, and burning would provide the supplies and ammunition he needed. Then his band would flee back north before the Army could be sent to round them up. The situation had become worse with the passing months. There was terror again on the northern frontier.

Miles was determined to trap the wily Sioux chief on a foray over the border and bring him back to Fort Keogh. He knew he had to act before his real intentions were known to either the Indians or the authorities in Washington. Otherwise he was certain to receive orders which would make it impossible for him to march against Sitting Bull.

> "We're marching off for Sitting Bull
> And this is the way we go—
> Forty miles a day, on beans and hay,
> With the Regular Army, O!"

Nelson Miles's deep voice led the singing as officers and men of his mounted column left Fort Peck on the Milk River in July of 1879. A strong detachment of the Second Cavalry, his own Fifth Infantry mounted on captured Indian ponies, packtrains, wagons, and a band comprised the force that was headed toward the Canadian border. Little Wolf and Brave Wolf, two Cheyenne chiefs who were now friendly to the general, rode well in advance of the column as scouts.

As the song said, forty miles a day was good time in this rough, drab country north of the Milk River. It was hard going in many ways, even for hardened veterans. The mounted infantry rode their captured Indian ponies almost like cavalrymen now. They were as accustomed to the saddle as to marching in heavy walking boots.

But the mosquitoes! The little insects pestered the men and horses day and night. They attacked in such clouds that it was almost impossible to keep them off. Hands and faces were swollen in great red welts where a dozen mosquitoes had attacked at a time. The nights were worst, Miles discovered, for then the only way to keep off the insects was to wrap one's head in a blanket. In July weather, one nearly smothered.

The winding column reached the camp of the Assiniboins, a tribe of the Sioux supposedly friendly with the whites. Miles called a parley with Old Necklace, their chief, a tall, ugly old Sioux. After exchanging the peace pipe and paying compliments, Miles turned again to the chief. "Give me warriors, Necklace, to fight your old enemy, Sitting Bull," he said.

Old Necklace's shrewd black eyes almost closed as he squinted under lowered lids. He hesitated a long time before replying. "We will give you twenty warriors, Bear Coat, to show our great loyalty to the Great White Father in Washington," the interpreter quoted for him. "And I hope you will have a good time in the north, for the Sioux up there are like the grass."

"And, chief," Miles replied, slowly and deliberately, "like the grass, we shall burn them up."

Whatever Old Necklace felt at this rebuke and open threat he kept to himself. But Miles went north with only twenty warriors of the Assiniboins to help in the fighting.

One morning not long afterward, the scouts reported that Indians were camped nearby. Miles deployed his mounted troops and artillery and charged. The Sioux, taken by surprise, fled before the bursting shells of the field guns, but Sitting Bull was able to lead his men over the border, where Miles could not pursue.

Again the Royal Northwest Mounted Police promised Miles they would keep a sharp eye on their unwanted visitor. There was nothing Miles could do but turn around and return to Fort Keogh.

The march northward nonetheless had been worthwhile, for the Sioux made no more raids below the border. They were too closely watched now by the Mounties. It was the last contact Miles had with Sitting Bull for a long time.

Fort Keogh had become maintenance headquarters for a big area of the frontier. After his return from the expedition against Sitting Bull, Miles was busy making it an even stronger post. More troops were assigned to him.

Then in November, 1880, after eleven years in command of the Fifth Infantry, Miles at last was promoted to the rank of brigadier general in the Regular Army. Even General Sherman could no longer withhold his approval of his nephew-in-law's new rank. The promotion was long overdue. Lesser men had been given preference while Miles was doing the real work of cleaning up the northern frontier. Between 1874 and 1880, Nelson Miles had brought peace to an area of more than 400,000 square miles, opening it up to settlement, the building of railroads, the opening of mines, and laying out of ranchlands.

Now the Army needed a man for a new job. Miles's promotion brought him a transfer to the command of the Department of the Columbia, an area that now includes the states of Oregon, Washington, Idaho, and Alaska.

The Indians of the northwest coast of the United States were very different from those of the Atlantic coast, the Great Lakes, and the Indians of the Plains and the Rocky Mountain regions. Usually the Pacific coast natives were more peaceful, but when aroused they could become fully as dangerous. Now the Northwest Indians were aroused. They were angry because of the same kind of injustices that had sent tribes to the east on the warpath.

The Columbia River basin had been settled, though sparsely, by highly industrious white men. Already they were rapidly developing the natural resources of the region —agriculture, mining, stock raising, lumber, and fisheries.

As in other parts of the United States, the onward march of civilization meant less room for the Indians to hunt and fish. The natives of the Northwest, like their fellows on the Plains, were being pushed out of the lands the government had promised they could keep forever. A strong hand and an understanding heart were needed to keep the peace, and Washington believed Miles was just the man to send. He had already made peace with more Indians than he had fought.

Nelson Miles, his wife, and their daughter arrived at his new post by steamer from San Francisco. They had gone west on the only transcontinental railroad built at that time.

The reputation of Bear Coat had preceded Miles to the Pacific coast. The Indians heard that he was not only a mighty warrior who could not be beaten, but that he was also a fair man whose word was good.

Miles plunged at once into the delicate business of trying to avert an Indian war. Within days he called in Chiefs Moses, Tonasket, Sarsopkin, and lesser chiefs for a peace talk. He heard their complaints, sifted out the most reasonable of them, and promised immediate recognition of the rights of their people. He could not guarantee that they would not be crowded further, but he did pledge that he would do all he could to prevent future injustices.

The chiefs quickly agreed that there should be no war. To make certain that his orders in their behalf were carried out, Miles put his most trusted aide, Major Frank D. Baldwin, in complete charge of the Indians in the entire department. The chiefs were sent to Washington to plead their own cause.

The arrangements that Miles made were so satisfactory

that never again was there the threat of an uprising among the natives of that part of the United States.

Miles's tour of duty in the Northwest was notable for several other achievements. He sent an aide-de-camp, Lieutenant Frederick Schwatka, to the eastern shore of Alaska and to the Yukon Valley. The party built a raft and floated 2000 miles down the Yukon. Later he sent Lieutenant W. F. Abercrombie to explore the valley of the Copper River, where no white men had successfully traveled. Years before, the Russians had two boatloads of men killed by natives during an attempt to explore the valley. The Russians gave up, but Abercrombie confirmed that there were untold mineral riches in Alaska beneath the frozen tundra.

Lieutenant Henry T. Allen floated 1500 miles down the Copper River the next spring under Miles's orders and aided surveyors who were working for railroads.

During the pleasant tour of duty a son was born to Nelson and Mary Miles, in Washington, December 5, 1882. They named the boy Sherman for his mother's family. Sherman followed his father and became a soldier, graduating from West Point and rising to the rank of major general in the United States Army.

Miles loved the Northwest for its scenery and its natural abundance, and for the challenge it gave to him to improve the condition of the people there, both white and Indian.

In July, 1885, President Grover Cleveland ordered Miles to command the Department of the Missouri with headquarters at Fort Leavenworth.

There was good reason for the sudden transfer. Trouble had broken out again in the Indian Territory—the same area where Miles had begun his real Indian fighting in 1874—and for much the same cause.

Indian lands had been leased to white cattlemen in direct violation of solemn treaties. The Indians were paid; but huge herds wandered over thousands of acres, and the natives knew they were receiving far less than the grazing rights were worth.

Lawless men moved into the area. There were frequent shootings. Indians were killed and little effort was made to bring anyone to justice. Many of the Indian camps became hangouts of outlaws. The Indians had protested, but in vain. Now they were threatening to take to the warpath again, even though their chiefs knew it would be suicide for their dwindling race to fight.

General Sheridan, commanding in Chicago, took Miles with him for talks with the chiefs of the Arapahoes, the Kiowas, the Comanches, and the Cheyennes. Most of these chiefs were known personally to both Sheridan and Miles, and the talks proved successful. War was averted because President Cleveland and General Sheridan approved Miles's plan to end the cattle leases. Miles put Captain Jesse M. Lee in charge of Indian affairs to make certain that the Army's new regulations were enforced. The troops which Miles had been quietly gathering were sent back to their posts just as quietly. He recommended a plan by which the Indians could provide for themselves by growing food and raising cattle with Federal help. The plan was approved in

Washington, and the natives were contented. Miles had averted another Indian war, one which was much closer to "civilization."

Sometimes it seemed that whenever there was trouble on the frontier, the first thing those in authority in Washington did was "send for Miles."

Within less than a year, it happened again.

SEVEN

GERONIMO!

THE Apache Indians had roamed at will for centuries through the area now embracing the states of Arizona and New Mexico, and part of northern Mexico. They had been at war with the white man ever since the days of the Spanish Conquest.

The Apaches believed themselves to be a superior race. They had always excelled in cunning, endurance, and cruelty. It was said that some of their warriors, even in the nineteenth century, could run a hundred miles in a single day. Once the Apaches had been numerous and powerful. In the spring of 1886 they were decimated by war, pestilence, and capture by white men. So greatly reduced were

171

they in numbers that their threat to the rapidly growing white civilization of the Southwest lay chiefly in the cunning of their daring, ruthless, surprise raids.

General Crook, whom the Apaches called Mantan Lupan, the Gray Wolf, was fighting them again. He was a brilliant officer, a veteran of the Civil War and of many Indian campaigns. He had won a splendid reputation, and Sherman, the general-in-chief, thought highly of him. Crook had preceded Miles by ten years on the frontier. During most of Miles's service in the West he had regarded Crook as his chief rival for promotion. Far too often, Miles had been outspoken in his criticism of the older man, feeling that he could have done any one of Crook's jobs better and quicker himself. His animosity had been fed by his belief that Crook was being preferred because he was a West Pointer. There is no evidence that this was so, but the conviction accounts for much of Miles's bitterness.

Crook was aging now, and far from well as a result of so much campaigning. He had done his job rounding up bands of Apaches before, but in trying to make a final cleanup and put an end to terror he was pitted against a ruthless and cunning Apache.

Geronimo, of the Chiricahua Apaches, had been a "bad" Indian ever since anyone on the Southwestern frontier could remember. Natchez was the hereditary chief of the Chiricahuas, but he took orders from the dominating Geronimo. Squat and dark-skinned, Geronimo had a full face with high cheekbones and a mouth that was almost a straight line. Geronimo's eyes were the eyes of a man at once ruthless, cunning, bold, and imaginative. His clothes were a combination of Indian garb and uniforms purloined from murdered soldiers. He wore a long knife at his belt and usually carried a long-barreled, single-shot rifle.

With several lesser chiefs, Geronimo had been leading Crook a merry chase over hundreds of square miles of arid land for many months. The Apaches of the badlands were well supplied with arms and ammunition from their many raids on stores, railroad freight trains, and lonely ranches. They would lie in wait for prospectors, miners, and ranchers, sometimes for days. They could subsist, if they had to, on very little food and water. Then they would strike, and seldom was anyone left alive to tell what had happened. It might be weeks before Mantan Lupan learned that his old enemy had struck again.

If hard pressed by Crook's troops, the Apaches would flee to the mountains. There they could live for days on field mice and the juice of the cactus. Almost always, however, Geronimo had been able to keep a good-sized camp well supplied with more palatable food and good forage for his animals. The camp was known to be in the Sierra Madre Mountains of northern Mexico, but to have sent troops in after the Indians would have been to risk the massacre of every man.

From time to time the Apaches would declare themselves peaceable and ride into their agencies and reservations to spend the winter quietly. In the spring, they would steal horses and what they needed from the agency store and escape to begin another campaign of robbing and killing. It was almost impossible to catch up with them; they were masters of the art of disguise and of evasion.

Raids, robbery, and murder. It was always the same pattern with Geronimo. In the spring of 1883 he had left a trail 300 miles long in Arizona. Crook's soldiers were almost helpless trying to fight him because they were forced to waste so many days following false trails. Crook finally trapped Geronimo in the mountains, and the old chief sent word down to the desert that he was ready to surrender. This time, he said, he meant it. So Crook with a troop of cavalry and 200 friendly Indian scouts met Geronimo on May 31, 1883, near Mascouri, just over the border in Mexico.

They were tired of the warpath, Geronimo told Crook when they met under a flag of truce. The old men, women, and children could go back to the San Carlos reservation at once. The warriors would gather up the livestock ranging in the mountains and report to San Carlos in two months.

Crook agreed, well pleased at such an easy settlement after so long and fruitless a pursuit. Two months passed, but by the end of that time Geronimo and his warriors were far away. They had resumed their raiding, robbing, and killing.

On March 14, 1884, Geronimo and fifteen of his band rode meekly into San Carlos and surrendered their ponies and guns. In return they received new blankets, food, and the freedom of the reservation. General Crook gave them some good advice instead of placing them in ankle irons.

It seemed that this time Geronimo really had reformed. At least Crook hoped so, but he took no unusual precautions to see that the chief did not escape.

The rest of Geronimo's warriors straggled into the reservation, a few at a time, and all were treated well instead of being arrested and tried as thieves and murderers. Crook hoped that this time Geronimo's people were tired of the warpath.

Then, on the night of May 17, 1885, Geronimo, Natchez, Chiahuahua, and fourteen warriors decided to hit the trail again for Mexico. They stole horses, guns and ammunition, and supplies and hurriedly left the reservation.

When their stealthy departure was discovered, Crook tried to send out word by telegraph to have troops round them up. What Crook didn't know was that the telegraph wire had been efficiently cut just outside the reservation. Geronimo had ordered one of his band to climb a cottonwood tree through which the line was strung and hack the strand with his short axe. Then the two ends were secured with a rawhide thong so that from the ground the wire seemed to be intact. The alarm for the fugitives was twenty-four hours late because troopers took that much time to locate the cut ends of the wire after the telegraph operator at San Carlos reported his line dead.

Within days Crook placed armed guards at every water hole in the vast area. The mountain passes were watched.

Special telegraph wires were strung so troops could be summoned more quickly from one area to another in an effort to trap the band.

It was no use.

In the fall of 1885 Geronimo's band slipped through Crook's network and traveled 1200 miles in New Mexico in five weeks. They killed thirty-eight persons, stole two hundred horses and cattle, again evaded the troops, and returned to the Sierra Madres to hole up for the winter.

Again Crook met Geronimo, and the chief agreed to surrender. Again he eluded the troops and resumed his raiding and killing. Crook sent some of the captured Apaches to Florida, but Geronimo, Natchez, and the other warriors remained at large. Two hundred Apache warriors led 3000 troops on a long series of wild-goose chases.

Crook finally gave up. On April 1, 1886, he asked to be relieved of his command. The following day Nelson Miles was transferred from the Department of the Missouri to command the Department of Arizona with headquarters in Fort Bowie, Arizona.

In all the years he had been on the frontier Miles never had known one Indian who broke faith when he gave his word, but having followed Crook's campaigns in Arizona and New Mexico, he was convinced that Geronimo could not be trusted under any circumstances. He was the most ruthless marauder the frontier ever had known. He and his remaining warriors had to be run down and exterminated or captured and sent to a distant reservation.

Miles's joy at having a chance to clean up the Southwest

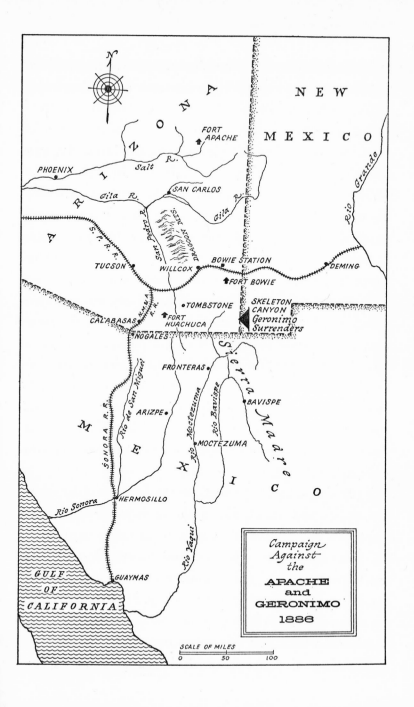

Campaign
Against
the
APACHE
and
GERONIMO
1886

was tempered by the knowledge that he had again been passed over for promotion. His old Civil War commander, General Oliver Otis Howard, and his longtime friend, General Alfred Terry, had been promoted to major generalcies as vacancies occurred. President Cleveland relied on seniority, despite the personal and written pleas of General Francis Barlow, who had been the first to recognize Miles's ability as a young lieutenant in the second year of the Civil War. Many other influential friends joined Barlow in urging the President to give Miles one of the vacancies on merit, regardless of seniority. Sheridan was quoted as saying, "In fact, Miles is the only man who amounts to anything, and on whom we can count, and I told the President and the Secretary so. . . ."

Despite his disappointment, Miles felt that it was fortunate that Sheridan had succeeded Sherman on the latter's retirement as general-in-chief. Sheridan, Miles knew, had often been annoyed by his persistence, but Sheridan, too, had learned that Miles was usually right. On the whole the two men hit it off well.

The aging General Howard was the new commander of the Division of the Pacific. Since the Department of Arizona was a part of this division, Miles technically would be junior to Howard. Miles was determined, however, that since the responsibility for cleaning up the Apaches was his, he alone would make the decisions. He would conduct his campaign in his own way.

Several weeks after his appointment to command the Department of Arizona with instructions to capture

Geronimo dead or alive, staff officers and unit commanders from all posts in his new district were called for a council of war. The personal staff Miles had brought with him from Fort Leavenworth consisted of one man, who of course knew his dynamic character firsthand. But the other officers at Fort Bowie knew him by reputation as a man who got things done. They knew he had initiative, audacity, and imagination. Their zeal was fired by the prospect of serving under him.

Nelson Miles stood in front of a large-scale map of Arizona and New Mexico at his Fort Bowie headquarters.

"Geronimo cuts the telegraph lines," he said. "Let's see how good he is at blotting out the sun's rays. We shall depend for communications chiefly upon the heliograph. We shall not rely upon the telegraph."

There were quick understanding nods of approval and broad grins as the officers realized the simplicity and effectiveness of Miles's plan.

The principle of the heliograph was not new. It had been used by the Algerians and others as early as the eleventh century. Mirrors reflected the sun's rays, and the reflection could be regulated by shading the mirror. Messages were sent in dot and dash code. Since the reflected rays could be seen a long distance, two groups of men, stationed on different hills, could "talk" to one another. The constantly fair weather and clean air of the Southwest would be perfect for the heliograph. "From one of these high buttes we can send a signal for 200 miles or more by using sunlight," the general added.

Best of all, there was no way Geronimo could stop communications unless he captured all of the heliograph instruments. A strong force at each signal point could prevent that. Miles now had more than 5000 troops, so there would be enough men to guard the heliograph stations and for service in the field, too.

Miles's first general order provided for the division of the area into military districts with heliograph stations, troops, and supplies for each. Each command could operate independently of the others and of headquarters, but would be in contact at all times.

If Indians were discovered in one district, they were to be pursued and captured or destroyed by the command in that district. If reinforcements were needed in any district, or if the Indians crossed over the line into another district, headquarters was to be informed. Necessary steps would be taken to keep the pursuit going. Always, by day or night, and regardless of the men and the horses, a command was to pursue any band of Indians it sighted until reinforced or relieved.

"This simple plan," the general explained, "is the same one used many years ago to capture wild horses in Texas. It was very successful, and so shall we be."

Then began the most terrible experience in the savage career of Geronimo.

Captain Henry W. Lawton of the Fourth Cavalry, a veteran of the Civil War and of the Indian frontier wars, was chosen to lead an expedition of 100 picked men into Mexico itself. To the command of Captain Lawton was assigned Assistant Surgeon Leonard Wood, fresh out of Harvard Medical School. Only a few years later Wood was to command the Rough Riders in the Spanish American War.

Lawton did not have long to wait. Geronimo raided in southwest Arizona, then hit the trail for Mexico. Lawton's command was ready the instant the heliograph message was received.

"We don't know just where Geronimo's band is at the moment," Miles explained to Lawton as the captain was starting out from Fort Bowie on his mission, "but I suspect he is somewhere south of the border. We know he holes up in some valley in the Sierra Madres. Be careful. Never let Geronimo surprise you, and never let him get too close to you!"

The captain waved acknowledgment of the advice and was gone in a rising cloud of yellow, alkaline dust. Miles did not see Lawton for a long time. The captain was on his own in a vast, arid wilderness, pitting his skill and endurance against one of the most cunning Indians ever known in the Southwest.

Other commands also took up the chase. The plan was to envelop the Apaches in a widely spread net of troops.

During the next few months there were frequent encounters between the Apaches and the cavalry. Indians were constantly pursued, and this time they could not throw off the troops so easily as in the past. Almost as fast as one command lost the trail, another picked it up, thanks to the heliograph. The fresh command followed immediately, giving the Indians no rest and, indeed, little time to eat or sleep.

In every fight with the troops the Apaches were defeated, but still they managed to slip away, sometimes with heavy losses. Pursuit followed an irregular, sometimes crisscross, path over New Mexico, Arizona, and old Mexico. The Mexican authorities cooperated fully with Miles's men. They were as anxious to get rid of Geronimo as the Americans were.

During the months of hard campaigning, Miles covered many hundreds of miles himself on horseback. The region was one of the most desolate of the world and the worst in which he had ever fought. He thought it more forbidding than the Staked Plains of New Mexico and Texas or the desolate region he had campaigned in far to the north. The illusion of distance, or rather, of nearness, always fooled him, as it did any newcomer to this wild land of glaring colors and unearthly bright sunshine. The air was so dry and clear and the sun so strong that distant objects always seemed much closer than they were. He had to allow constantly for the phenomenon in his calculations.

Then one day Lawton picked up a fresh trail that led his command by forced marches some 200 miles into old Mexico, to the Yaqui River country. Food was low and water had to be strictly rationed for both men and horses. Nowhere was there game to be shot for food.

For three months Lawton pursued Geronimo's Apaches over rough mountain country. The Indians tried every ruse they could devise. Frequently they abandoned their horses and crossed some of the most rugged mountains on the continent on foot. They jumped from rock to rock, hoping their trail would be lost, but the keen eyes of Lawton's loyal Indian scouts always picked up the trail again.

One morning after a sharp brush with a band of Geronimo's men who had tried to ambush him in a narrow canyon, Captain Charles A. Hatfield captured one of the chief's wounded braves. The captain sent the man under guard over the long trail to Fort Bowie.

Miles questioned the Apache closely through an interpreter when he was well enough. He had been seriously wounded, but he seemed willing to talk.

Geronimo's men, the warrior told Miles, were worn down after five months of hot pursuit by the bluecoats. They had no food. And they could not travel far without water. They had no rest, no time to hunt for food. Never had they been chased so far or so fast.

When Miles asked if Geronimo and the men were ready to surrender, the Apache nodded. Miles wondered if the man was just trying to please him, or whether there might be some truth in what he indicated.

"Our men are exhausted," went on the Apache. "Our animals are in even worse condition. Food and water are scarce. For the first time since I can remember we are discouraged."

The brave spoke with something almost like a sigh, as much expression as an Indian ever permitted himself. Miles could believe what the man said was true. It was the way he had planned his campaign against Geronimo. But he remembered also that the wily leader of the Chiricahua Apaches had surrendered many times to Crook, and had then gone back to robbing and killing.

When the man was well enough to travel, Miles sent him back to Geronimo's camp beyond the peaks of the Sierra Madres with a message.

Captain Lawton himself, meanwhile, had opened long-range talks with Geronimo through a runner from the Indian camp in the hidden valley.

"I will surrender only to the highest authority," Geronimo told Lawton. He meant he would give himself up only to Miles. Geronimo never had trusted white men, but he knew Bear Coat's word was good.

Geronimo backed up his offer to surrender by sending his brother to Fort Bowie as hostage. That was enough evidence of good faith for Miles, although he still did not trust Geronimo. He rode down to Skeleton Canyon, near the border, to join Lawton's hard-bitten command. Around him in the lush valley lay the bleached bones of many white men who had been massacred over the years by the Apaches.

Geronimo was camped not far away. The next day he rode into Miles's camp with as much dignity as he could muster. It was his first meeting with the general, although he knew the legend of Bear Coat and the saying among the Indians that no bullet could touch him.

The morning breeze which precedes the hot hours of the day in many parts of the Southwest stirred the flag and ruffled the cavalry guidons. Already the rocks were absorbing the terrific heat which soon would be reflected back onto all living things.

Geronimo, dirty, ill-kept, his long hair stringy and soiled from much exposure to the elements, was a strange contrast to the dusty and travel-stained but otherwise immaculately uniformed Miles.

"Geronimo is ready to return to Fort Apache with the great Bear Coat," the chief announced through an interpreter.

Miles shook his head. "You will have to come back with me to Fort Bowie," he replied. "There no longer are any Indians at Fort Apache."

Geronimo was surprised and showed it. "Where are they?"

"I have sent most of the other Apache tribes east on the iron horse, many days' travel away. There they will live in peace. They will not be able to rob and murder as they have done for so long here."

"Then," haggled Geronimo, "at least permit us to keep our ponies and our arms."

Again the general shook his head. "No, Geronimo. Your ponies and your guns are stolen anyway. They are not yours. You may ride the ponies to Fort Bowie; then you will surrender them to me. You will give up your guns to me now."

Geronimo hesitated before asking his next question. He took a long, appraising look at the tall, uncompromising officer. He missed the easy-going Mantan Lupan, whom he had deceived so many times over the years. It had been much easier to do business with Crook. "What will be my fate, and that of my men, if we accept your surrender terms, Bear Coat?"

Miles's blue eyes did not relent a shade. Geronimo was pleading now, something he had probably never done in his life, but the general felt no sense of satisfaction. He did realize that things were beginning to go his way, after all. "Your fate will be up to the Great White Father in Washington. He alone can determine what is to be done to you."

Geronimo shrugged, somewhat defiantly, Miles thought, and again he wondered if the chief would change his mind.

A heliograph had been set up on a butte near the camp. More than fifty miles away, on a mountain peak, another heliograph detachment was stationed. It was a bright, clear day, perfect for sending sun messages. The general had a sudden inspiration. He turned again to Geronimo in his most persuasive manner. "Your brother is hostage to us at Fort Bowie, Geronimo, sixty-five miles away, a day and a half on horseback. Watch these soldiers with the mirrors. They will send any message you like to your brother. And you will get an answer from him within a few minutes."

Geronimo grunted, thought a long minute, then suggested, "Ask my brother how he fares at Fort Bowie."

Miles relayed the message to the heliograph team on the nearby butte. The heliograph flashed a series of dots and dashes. Then the signaling stopped, and the little group at the parley in the center of Miles's camp waited for some time. It was evident that Geronimo did not believe he would receive an answer.

Suddenly from the distant peak came a series of bright flashes. "Look!" Miles said. He handed his field glasses to Geronimo and quickly showed him how to use them.

An aide brought the written message to Miles, and it was translated to Geronimo. He nodded slowly in wonder. "The message truly was from my brother in Fort Bowie," he agreed. "I know, for he told me not only that he is being well treated, but added a word the meaning of which only he and I have known from childhood."

Geronimo stared at Miles in complete amazement. For once his composure broke, and he allowed all to see how impressed he had been by the sun messages.

"You could cut the telegraph wires of the Gray Wolf," Miles reminded him grimly, "but you cannot blot out the rays of the sun. By means of those rays Bear Coat can send messages in seconds farther than your horses can travel in more than a day."

The look of stark amazement was still on Geronimo's seamed, dark face. Then something almost like a smile curved his hard lips. "So that is the manner by which you have sent messages these many moons! We never suspected how it was done."

Miles nodded. He had intended to impress Geronimo, and he knew now that his plan had worked. Geronimo had been in no position to dictate the terms he would accept, but he needed to be made to realize it. But could the chief persuade Natchez and the other Apaches to come in from their mountain retreat and surrender? Without the hereditary chief of the Chiricahua Apaches, Geronimo's surrender might not end the danger to the frontier.

"We have known where you and your men were most of the time for the past five months," Miles told Geronimo. "We did not depend upon the 'whispering wire' to send messages. You cannot fight us longer, for even the sun battles on our side."

Slowly Geronimo nodded in agreement, but the fierce glint in his hard, black eyes showed how reluctantly the words were forced from him. "It is so, Bear Coat. I can fight you no longer."

Geronimo turned to a warrior and barked a guttural order. An Indian interpreter at once translated it for the general. Geronimo was sending word to Chief Natchez of what he had seen. He was telling him to come in with all the band at once to surrender to Bear Coat. "The white man's magic is too powerful."

Natchez obeyed Geronimo's order at once and rode in with the rest of the band.

The next day Miles, escorted by a troop of cavalry, rode the sixty-five miles to Fort Bowie in a forced march with Geronimo, Natchez, and four of the lesser chiefs. He left the remainder of the command to bring in the captive warriors. He was taking no chances that the Apaches might change their minds about surrendering.

As the dusty file of cavalrymen and their prisoners rode through the heavy gates of Fort Bowie, Miles motioned with one hand to a lieutenant. The officer rode back along the column to the point where Geronimo, Natchez, and the lesser chiefs were closely guarded by specially picked troopers. The lieutenant spoke fluent Apache, which is why he had been picked for the assignment. There must be no mistaking Miles's order.

Geronimo looked at the young officer in surprise, then craned his neck trying to look ahead to where Miles sat his horse without once looking back.

"But," protested Geronimo, almost sputtering, "I have returned to Fort Bowie willingly. I have surrendered. What do you want of me, except to show me to my quarters and provide me with nourishment?"

"Come with me," replied the lieutenant, ignoring the question. The detail of guards turned their horses, nosing the Indian ponies so hard that the order had to be obeyed.

The little group stopped in front of Miles. Geronimo, by now, suspected that all was not as he had expected it to be.

"You are now prisoners of the United States. You will be well treated, as I have promised. But you will be placed under heavy guard. And do not think that you can escape. Your guards will have orders to shoot to kill any prisoner who tries to leave Fort Bowie."

Geronimo started to protest angrily, but Miles cut him short. "This time, Geronimo, you may consider yourself fortunate that I do not put you in the shackles that once bound your legs at San Carlos. But I shall see to it that you do not escape. You are going to be sent far, far away, with the rest of the Apache nation."

Miles felt relief and great satisfaction. He had accomplished his mission, and he did not intend to give Geronimo any chance to get away. It had happened too many times already. Geronimo was a brutal killer and should be dealt with as such.

Geronimo, Natchez, and the other chiefs were locked up securely in special cells, still vehemently protesting. Double guards were posted. The garrison was put on the alert for trouble, but none came. Three days later Captain Lawton rode in with the rest of the Apaches. These, too, were securely locked up. Now there was no force of hostiles loose in either Arizona or New Mexico that was big enough or strong enough to attempt a rescue if Geronimo changed his mind.

Then, on a sunny day in the late fall, while the band played "Auld Lang Syne," the Apaches, led by Geronimo and Natchez, were escorted to a special train and shipped to Mount Vernon, Alabama, and exile.

One small band, led by Chief Mangus, was chased for several weeks by troops under Captain Charles L. Cooper, but it was finally captured and the Indians were sent away.

In five months Nelson Miles had rid Arizona and New Mexico of the last of the Apaches—a job other generals had failed to do in many hard-fought campaigns over the years.

While in Arizona Miles discovered the richness of the soil when it had sufficient water. On the picket line oats were often spilled while the horses were being fed. Usually the dusty soil of that area grew only cactuslike plants that require little moisture, but now and then, when enough water happened to soak the ground, a near-miracle occurred within a few days. Oats seeded themselves and shoots of tender green leaves came through the parched, dusty soil.

Not many such incidents were needed to set the general thinking what a different face the country would present if it were possible to irrigate the land. The same was true of other sections of the Southwest where he had been, in Texas and New Mexico and in arid regions of California.

Miles wrote an article for the *North American Review* in 1890 in which he suggested that the Federal government help in water storage and irrigation. He followed up his suggestion by pressing for irrigation every chance he had. His plan was not adopted for more than a dozen years. Then the government began to plan for irrigation. The general had anticipated its vast benefits to agriculture. He was a famous soldier, but he had not forgotten his training as a farm boy back in Massachusetts. He still loved the land, and he looked at it with a farmer's eye.

The people of Arizona were enthusiastically grateful for Miles's successful campaign against the Apaches. At a dinner in his honor in Tucson, with Mary at his side, in December, 1887, the people presented a sword to him. It had been specially designed by Tiffany's in New York and had a fifty-six carat sapphire embedded in the hilt. The gold scabbard was engraved with stirring scenes from the campaign against Geronimo.

In accepting the honor, Miles of course gave his officers and men a big share of credit for the successful outcome of the venture. He didn't stop with praise of his men. He urged better pay and food for them, and suggested to Washington that the men be spared unnecessary duty. He proposed a plan by which officers long on the frontier might receive promotion without waiting so many years for it when it was well deserved. Some of his superiors might be jealous of him, and some might still think him rash, but since the first days of his service as a lieutenant in the Massachusetts Infantry, Miles had always looked after the welfare of his men. Strict though he was, the soldiers knew that he always did his best for them, and they loved and respected him for it.

It wasn't long, however, before Miles's lack of tact got him into trouble again. At a dinner in San Francisco in 1888, where he then commanded, he was mentioned as a possible candidate for President. He didn't bother to deny a lack of ambition in that direction, and at once his silence invited attack by the opposition. He was denounced by some Eastern newspapers, and there was a hue and cry from politicians. The excitement soon died down, however, when it was seen that Miles really was not interested —at least not too much—in running for President. He had only two loves, Mary and soldiering.

General Terry retired and the vacant major generalcy went to Crook. Then Crook died suddenly on March 21, 1890. Miles, as senior brigadier general, believed he should have the promotion to major general. He was supported by prominent Pacific coast citizens, but Senator John Sherman, Mary's influential uncle, wrote to Miles that he didn't think President Cleveland would appoint him. The President thought Miles "if not disobedient, at least a troublesome man to get along with."

Miles, who was in the East at the time, took the next train to Washington, asked for and received an appointment with the President, stated his case, and in less than an hour won the major generalcy. He was to be transferred back to his old post at Fort Leavenworth as commander of the Department of the Missouri. Direct, forceful action had won again!

Mary was not in Washington with him at the time, and he wrote to her that all he needed to complete his happiness was to hold "my own darling in my arms."

EIGHT

THE GHOST DANCERS

AFTER his roundup of the remaining Apache brigands Miles had hoped that he had seen the last Indian war. There had been peace on the frontier for a long time, but once again, dishonest white agents and contractors had stirred the natives to desperation. The Sioux were starving on their lands in North and South Dakota.

Bad food, poor equipment, brutal treatment—it was a list of grievances which no one in Washington would act upon. Miles had done his best, but powerful influences opposed his plans for the proper care of the Indians on their reservations.

Unknown to the military, trouble was in the making in

the badlands of Nevada. The Indians of the Northwest had kept the secret of the Ghost Dancers well.

Wovoka, a Piute Indian medicine man who called himself the Messiah, had appeared among the tribes. He told them he would lead them eastward to regain their lost lands, that as they marched toward the rising sun, their dead warriors would rise up into new life, fully armed and mounted, and fight beside them to take back the lands the white man had stolen.

In part his wild story was based upon what the Indians had been taught of the Christian religion; part of it was strictly pagan in origin; and all of it was calculated to appeal to Indian imagination and superstition. The promise the Messiah held out to the savages traveled through the tribes on their agencies with the speed of the wind.

In 1889 three prominent chiefs had traveled westward to talk with Wovoka. Kicking Bear was well known to Miles. Tall and stalwart, the man was a natural leader with some of the magnetism of Sitting Bull himself. Short Bull was a small, sharp-featured dreamer, much better at exhorting his people to action than at leading them in battle. Porcupine, a keen, wiry, little Indian had always been a bitter enemy of all white men, and he was a most persuasive talker.

During their visit with the Messiah, they had been taught the mysteries of the new religion the Piute preached. Later they made their way back some 1200 miles to the Standing Rock reservation in North Dakota. On their way they told the story of the Messiah and his promise to every Indian who would listen. Most of them did.

What worried Miles most was the Ghost Dance, a strange rite invented by the Messiah. He had seen it in all its frenzy on an inspection trip to South Dakota. He had warned the Indians at that time that they must stop performing it, for he knew how excited they could become. They had listened sullenly, but the dance continued after he left the reservation.

The Indians wore a ghost shirt for the dance and threw dust over their shoulders. The ritual was supposed to turn the white man's bullets from their bodies. Together with a weird, warlike, almost hypnotic chant, the dance was stirring even ordinarily peaceful tribes into a frenzy.

Some time before, the Canadian authorities had made it plain they would no longer have Sitting Bull in their territory. He had returned to the United States promising to behave. Now the story of the Ghost Dancers aroused his lifelong hatred of the white man once again with greater fury than ever. Whether or not he really believed the story told by the Piute no one knows; probably he thought it was a good chance for a last crusade against the whites. In any case, Sitting Bull decided to join forces with the Messiah. He pictured himself as the leader of the uprising, as he had been in so many other struggles against the white man.

Sitting Bull sent runners to all the tribes; the fighting men were to meet him at the base of the Rocky Mountains at a spot he would choose. From there they would march westward to meet the Messiah. They would have enough food, he assured them. Instead of buffalo, which the white man had driven from the plains, they would kill cattle for beef. There would be plenty of arms and ammunition, for they would rob stores in the small towns along the way. Horses and ponies they would steal from ranchers and small farmers.

Miles knew that if Sitting Bull and the Messiah joined forces, a new and terrible Indian war might result. The whole frontier, now becoming settled and prosperous, might erupt into flaming terror.

As always in an emergency, the general took the field at once. He set up field headquarters in Rapid City, South Dakota, the city nearest the probable scene of action. It was not too far from the badlands, toward which most of the hostiles were known to be moving.

There were many famous Indian chiefs in the great conspiracy. Besides Kicking Bear, Short Bull, and Porcupine, the chiefs Two Strike, Big Foot, and Hump, whom Miles had fought in Montana and later had taken on as a scout, were also leading their people to join the insurrection.

Miles appealed to Chief Hump, who readily agreed to lead his people back to their reservation. Some of the other chiefs at once followed his example, but by early autumn of 1890, Sitting Bull had not recalled the message he had sent to every tribe in the Northwest. The Minneconjoux, the Sans Arcs, the Oglalas, Cheyennes, Brules, Gros Ventres, Yanktonais, the Fiegans, and the Mandans were set to march against the white community. The latter two tribes usually were friendly to the whites, but they, too, were gyrating in frenzy to the savage rhythm of the Ghost Dance.

Miles knew he had to act quickly. If the Messiah and his disciples came east, Sitting Bull would have to be put where he could not lead another Indian war. Without him there likely would be little trouble.

"Arrest Sitting Bull!"

When the commanding officer at Fort Yates, North Dakota, received the terse order from Miles, he sent Major E. G. Fechet with a troop of cavalry and a company of loyal Indian police to bring Sitting Bull into the fort. Fechet was an officer with long experience in Indian warfare and well qualified for the job.

Sitting Bull's camp was only about thirty miles from Fort Yates. By a forced march, Major Fechet reached the vicinity of the camp during the night. He did not know it then, but had he arrived next day he would have been too late. Sitting Bull and well-armed and well-mounted warriors were ready to leave at dawn to join the tribesmen assembling on an almost inaccessible mesa in the badlands of South Dakota.

Fechet sent the Indian police into the camp to arrest Sitting Bull. The chief was aroused, protesting, from sleep. His warriors had performed the Ghost Dance on the eve of their new venture and all were asleep, worn to exhaustion by the frenzy of the dance. When it was explained that he was under arrest and must go at once to Fort Yates, he yelled defiance and struggled. In spite of his years he had great strength; several Indian policemen were needed to subdue him. His struggle was a short one, for his captors were too powerful. He was dragged from his cabin.

Suddenly he raised the fierce Sioux war cry. A shot was fired, but whether by one of the Sioux or by an Indian policeman no one knew. Armed warriors rushed to their chief's aid. Within seconds there was a general hand-to-hand struggle in the darkness. The night rang with war cries of the Sioux and the yells of Indian policemen. Fechet had to send in his troops to aid the police.

The Sioux warriors retreated to a strong position behind rocks, leaving Sitting Bull and many of his braves dead in the camp.

Miles knew that the danger of an uprising was not ended completely by the death of Sitting Bull. The Ghost Dance teachers had done their vicious work too well. Many of the Sioux, especially the young bucks, were inflamed to a pitch that could only be satisfied by bloodshed.

In their zeal to follow the glory road back to power, most of the Indians had burned their lodges and destroyed their recently harvested crops. They had left the security of their reservations and agencies, such as it was, to take to the warpath. They faced starvation in the reservations anyway, so the dangers and privations of such a march did not frighten them. The poor seed given to them had yielded far less food than they needed for the cold months.

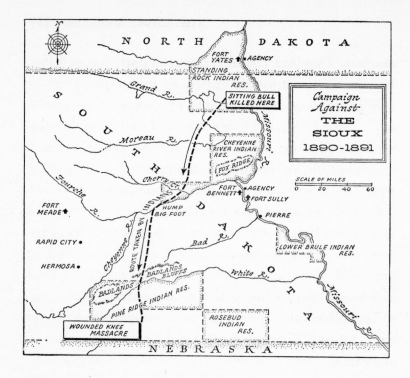

Campaign
Against
THE
SIOUX
1890-1891

They lacked good meat as well. Suffering had led them to accept the Messiah in the first place.

Old men, women, and children rode or walked with the warriors, carrying their pitifully few belongings and tepees on pony-drawn travois, the long poles cutting deep furrows in the bare earth. They were headed for one of the most desolate regions of the West, the Dakota badlands. A mass of barren hills, narrow valleys, ravines, canyons, and buttes, the area was almost without trees or shrubs and had little grass. Wagons could not cross it, and even the sure-footed horses and ponies had to pick their way carefully over the rough, broken ground.

On the way to the place of meeting, the Indians could shoot elk, deer, or the domestic cattle of farmers and ranchers. They had a good supply of horses, ponies, rifles, and ammunition for their immediate needs.

Miles's plan was still to round up the tribesmen peacefully. Then he would replace agents of the Indian Bureau with trusted army officers. Before leaving his headquarters in Chicago for South Dakota, the general had set in motion a plan to provide good food and new seed for the Indians if he could get them back on their reservations. President Benjamin Harrison was in earnest agreement with him that every effort must be made to get the Indians back without bloodshed.

Miles's strategy required skill and tact. He deployed his troops so that they formed a great hollow square many miles in depth. There must be no shooting; even the threat of gunplay might stampede the hostiles into outright war. Instead, the Indians were to be herded by easy stages within a closing line of troops toward the center of the square, the Pine Ridge Indian Reservation in southwestern South Dakota.

Word of the death of Sitting Bull had spread fast. Many Indians who had been on the point of surrendering peacefully now thought better of it. They were afraid that they, too, would be killed without a chance to fight for their lives.

Big Foot fled with his band to Wounded Knee Creek in southwestern South Dakota. The cavalry finally caught up with him, surrounded his camp in bitter winter weather, and demanded his surrender. The troops outnumbered the Indians by almost four to one.

Miles's orders were to persuade Big Foot to come in and surrender, not to fight him if a battle could be avoided. This time he was not so fortunate in his choice of an officer to do a tactful job. Colonel James W. Forsythe of the Seventh Cavalry, which since the Custer massacre had hated all Indians, decided he would disarm the Sioux at once and ship them by the nearest railroad directly back to their reservation. He ordered a thorough search of Big Foot's camp, determined to make certain that no weapons were concealed there.

While the search was being carried out by a detail of troopers, an argument occurred. The Brules, thinking they were to be killed, as Sitting Bull had been, went into the frenzied Ghost Dance. They threw dust over their shoulders and sang the death song. They were prepared to die fighting. Instead of trying to calm them and attain their peaceful surrender, Forsythe continued his search for weapons.

Then, at a signal from Big Foot, the Brules made a rush for the guns they actually did have concealed. They began firing at the troops. Unfortunately, some of Forsythe's men had been stationed, against all tactical good sense, between the Indians and the camp. Within minutes the cavalrymen found themselves engaged in a pitched battle. There were heavy military losses, and a great massacre of Indians resulted. During the long chase after the battle the cavalry killed and wounded many more of Big Foot's warriors. Some of the Brules escaped to spread the story of Wounded Knee among the tribes still in the badlands.

Miles moved his headquarters to Pine Ridge after the massacre at Wounded Knee. He summarily removed Forsythe from command for permitting the incident to occur, but despite Miles's vigorous opposition, Forsythe was later restored to command after a court of inquiry heard the case in Washington. Miles never agreed with the decision and later he opposed Forsythe's promotion. In the Army in those days, it seemed that a man who killed Indians, no matter how brutally, often received more credit than an officer who tried to win without resorting to killing or trickery.

The latest massacre had aroused the fears of such chiefs as Broad Tail and Spotted Eagle. Miles knew each of them personally, as indeed he knew most of the chiefs in the Northwest.

Once again Miles tried to calm and reassure them. "I will be your friend and help you in Washington to get your treaties kept if you will surrender to me and follow my advice," he promised the chiefs.

Because the chiefs had learned over the years that if Bear Coat promised to help them he would do his best, they were inclined to go along with him. Still, remembering the brutal and senseless slaughter at Wounded Knee, they hesitated. The chiefs heard, for such news travels quickly, that Miles had removed Forsythe. His prompt action seemed to the Indians to be further assurance that Bear Coat meant them no harm. Chief Red Cloud, who had fought the whites even before Miles arrived on the frontier, was now at Pine Ridge with Chief American

Horse. These chiefs did all they could to persuade others
to surrender.

Days passed before the chiefs decided to accept Miles's
offer. They knew they were surrounded by troops, but
they were never conscious of more than a gentle pressure.
The troops, under Miles's strict orders, would camp in one
spot for a day or two, then break camp and move forward
a few miles. The Indians would retreat a little, pitch a new
camp, and wait.

Miles had provided his troops with warm winter clothing, as he had in his campaigns in Texas, New Mexico, and
Montana, but the Indians, many of them without shelter
and most of them with dwindling food and little wood for
their fires, were in pitiable condition. The temperature
held far below zero and the wind was cold and bitter.
There was snow and the streams were frozen.

Early in January, 1891, the last of the chiefs gave up.
The surrender was complete.

Miles was more determined than ever to help the Indians. Shelter, food, warm blankets, fuel, and other supplies were provided for their immediate needs. Only his
most trusted and experienced officers were placed in charge
of them. He was determined to see that his orders were
carried out to the letter.

Thirty of the most prominent Indians, including Kicking Bear and Short Bull, were sent to army headquarters
in Chicago as hostages. American Horse, Broad Tail, and
several other chiefs were sent to Washington to present
their claims in person to President Harrison. Captain Jesse

M. Lee was put in charge of all Indian agencies and reservations, and he was made personally responsible to General Miles.

The Messiah's plans for an Indian uprising were thoroughly blocked. He slipped quietly into the shadows and was never heard of again.

The last Indian war had been fought. It had taken Nelson Miles twenty-one years to clean up the frontier.

NINE

FIGHTER TO THE LAST

CHICAGO was swept by angry mobs in June, 1891, as a strike at the plant of the Pullman Company erupted into a general tieup. Trains, even those carrying the mail, were stopped.

President Grover Cleveland ordered Miles to Chicago at once. His orders were to restore order and to protect government property. The military action was not to be directed against the labor unions, only against lawless mobs and their leaders if they got out of hand.

By telegraph, Miles ordered picked troops in from every post in the country that could possibly spare them. He stripped many forts of all but caretaker garrisons, and he had the assurance of President Cleveland that units of the National Guard would be called out and sent to Chicago if they were needed.

Detachments of infantry, cavalry, and artillery arrived from many parts of the country. Quickly Miles deployed his regulars—most of them veterans of the Indian wars—at strategic points in the city. They would back up the police if they were needed, but after a few days the crisis passed. The local authorities had been able to work out their problems.

In October, 1894, Miles was promoted to commanding general of the Army, with headquarters in Washington. This post placed him second to the President in command of the Regular Army.

But in what a sad state he found his new command!

There were fewer than 50,000 soldiers in the Regular Army, and they were scattered in military posts all over the country. Few were in the coastal districts. The country had been so intent on holding Indians in check that little attention had been paid to areas where protection might be needed in case of war with an outside power.

The big guns of the coast defense artillery had long since become obsolete. Their range was not great enough to hit warships that might stand off the coast and bombard cities with new high-explosive shells. The defenses of the country were in dangerously poor condition.

General Miles had known most of these alarming facts before he became commanding general, of course, for he had a way of digging into reports and of anticipating events. Within a short time the Regular Army became a more effective fighting force. It was better equipped and ready for quick action in an emergency. Modernization of the coast defenses was begun. A similar remodeling was being done by the Navy, largely through the energetic action of the young Assistant Secretary of the Navy, Theodore Roosevelt.

America was teetering on the brink of war with Spain. As far back as 1854, the United States had tried to buy the island of Cuba, which had belonged to Spain since the days of Christopher Columbus. The natives had long been held in what amounted to slavery, and they had made many attempts to throw off the Spanish yoke, but without success. A new rebellion, led by the grizzled veteran fighter for freedom, General Iniguez Garcia, had been in progress for some time. So serious had the situation between Spain and the United States become that the USS *Maine* was sent to Havana to protect American citizens.

Miles still believed the trouble between the two countries could be arbitrated. Then an event occurred which took the matter out of everybody's hands. On the night of February 15, 1898, the *Maine* blew up in Havana harbor with great loss of American life.

"On to Havana!" screamed the newspaper headlines, although there was not then, and there is not now, evidence to prove that the tragedy was not an accident. "We must fight Spain!" shouted some congressmen. Within a short time there was an official declaration of war.

General Miles, as commander of the land forces of the United States, found himself in a critical situation. His small army would have to go to Cuba on transports, under the protection of the guns of the American Navy, but the Navy was not sure that it could defeat the Spanish fleet.

Hotheads in Congress urged the immediate invasion of Cuba, but largely due to Miles, this foolish move was held off until the naval supremacy in Cuban waters could be decided.

Then Admiral George Dewey and a small American squadron sank the Spanish Asiatic fleet in the harbor of Manila in the Philippines. The United States at last realized its strength on the sea.

Part of the Spanish Navy was bottled up in the harbor of Santiago de Cuba by a small American squadron and was destroyed when it tried to escape. Spain's sea power was crushed; Cuban waters at last were safe for American troop transports.

While waiting for a decisive naval engagement, Miles had been building up the Army. He gathered men from distant posts and equipped them. He supervised the raising of a volunteer army.

One of the volunteer commands was known as the Rough Riders, a cavalry unit commanded by Colonel Leonard Wood. Second in command was Lieutenant Colonel Theodore Roosevelt, who later was to become President.

The tactics to be employed in Cuba were essentially those which had worked so successfully in many of Miles's other campaigns. The Spanish force in Cuba and Puerto Rico would be cut in two and the stronger half, Cuba, attacked first. The rebels were strongest at the southern end of the island and could give the most help to American troops there.

There were many problems to be worked out before actual invasion, however, one of the most important of which was the deplorable condition of troops waiting in Florida to be transported to Cuba. The housing and food were bad, the equipment slow in arriving.

General William R. Shafter was sent to Cuba in command of the American Army to help Garcia, the Cuban patriot leader. The American Navy bottled up the island, preventing Spain from sending reinforcements or the Spanish garrison from fleeing. The Spaniards were trapped unless they could hold off the American invasion force. The Cuban people were against them almost to a man. There were sharp engagements, but no decisive results, and the Spaniards did not surrender.

Then Miles's primary fear for the success of the invasion was realized. Yellow fever broke out among the troops, most of whom were in no physical condition to fight in the heat and the fever-ridden jungles. General Shafter was ill. There had to be a decision on the field of battle before yellow fever, if not the Spaniards, defeated the American Army.

By July President McKinley became so alarmed at the rapidly worsening situation in Cuba that he ordered Miles to go to the island. Miles sailed at once with reinforcements.

After a council of war, such of the Army as still could fight was quickly redeployed. Then, with Shafter's troops and his own reinforcements set to storm Santiago de Cuba, and the American fleet standing by in the bay, Miles gave the Spanish general, José Toral, just twenty-four hours to lay down his arms.

Toral had no choice. He gave up. Within a short time the whole island of Cuba was in control of the United States.

An invasion force, supported by the American fleet, was sent to Puerto Rico. After only six sharp engagements the Spaniards surrendered.

The United States withdrew from Cuba three years later, holding only the important naval base at Guantanamo. Puerto Rico became a possession of the United States.

Although Nelson Miles had participated in his last war, he was not through fighting for causes in which he believed.

He had taken a strong stand against the overall conduct of the war by Secretary of War Russell Alexander Alger, especially the handling of supplies. Largely as the result of Miles's open accusations, President McKinley named a special board of inquiry. At one hearing Miles told of his discovery of badly refrigerated beef at a Florida staging center during the early days of the war. It was, he said, "what you might call embalmed beef." Ultimately an army board of inquiry found that the beef was, indeed, unfit for the use of troops in a tropical country.

Miles got into another dispute when he took sides with Commodore Winfield Scott Schley, who commanded the American squadron that wiped out the Spanish fleet under Admiral Cevera. Schley claimed that he should have had the credit. He was in actual command on the day of the battle, but the planning had been done by his superior, Admiral William T. Sampson. A naval court of inquiry upheld Sampson. Miles defended Schley, and so actually took sides against the board of inquiry. President Roosevelt rebuked Miles publicly at the White House for interfering.

These incidents were mere skirmishes, however, compared to the big battle that lay ahead.

More to get the outspoken Miles temporarily out of the country, apparently, than for any other reason, he was ordered on an inspection tour of the Philippines.

The United States had taken the Philippines from Spain, but a large segment of the native population still carried on the war against the new rulers. Miles was under instructions not to interfere in the conduct of the war, but he discovered that the American military forces sometimes resorted to the torture of insurgents to get information. Miles, incensed at such practices, ordered the immediate suspension of any kind of torture or forced confession. He had always held firm views on the treatment of prisoners of war, and he took an open stand in the Philippines without waiting to consult his superiors in Washington, the President and the Secretary of War.

Roosevelt and his Secretary of War, Elihu Root, backed the commanding general of the Army in the Philippines and told him to ignore Miles's order. Then Miles figuratively charged in at the gallop. The story leaked to the newspapers, and the press had a field day of sensationalism. The country was thoroughly aroused, and a board of inquiry was ordered to get the facts.

Eventually the inquiry board found that Miles's charges were true. Certain officers had been guilty of using torture to force prisoners to reveal secrets. Two Filipinos were found to have been whipped to death by American soldiers. Miles had not always won in his battles for the underdog, but this time he did. There was no more torture reported in the Philippines.

Miles gave one last illustration of his fiery spirit and indomitable courage when, shortly before his retirement, President Roosevelt issued a fitness order to all officers in the Army. Each one was ordered to make a horseback ride of 100 miles in three days. Miles, despite his age, set up a ten-mile horse relay between forts in the West and rode the entire 100 miles in one day! Only one of the several young officers who started with him completed the ride.

Miles was promoted to lieutenant general in 1900, but by that time the quest for rank and glory had somewhat dimmed in its appeal. There was little savor in the award.

He had gone to Japan and had been received in China by the dowager empress after his sensational stopover in the Philippines. He traveled to St. Petersburg, then the capital of Russia, where he was received by the czar. Paris and London gave him an almost royal welcome, for his fame as an Indian fighter now was well established all over the world.

On August 5, 1903, Nelson Miles retired from the Army.

Mary Miles died suddenly in 1904. Miles survived her for twenty-one years, but he never wholly recovered from the shock and grief of her death. His own came in May, 1925, and he was buried with full military honors in Arlington National Cemetery.

The finest tribute to this great soldier was written before his death by his chief scout—Colonel William F. (Buffalo Bill) Cody: "I have been in many campaigns with General Miles, and a better general and more gifted warrior I have never seen. I served in the Civil War and in any number of Indian wars; I have been under at least a dozen generals, with whom I have been thrown in close contact because of the nature of the services which I was called upon to render.

"I have known Phil Sheridan, Tecumseh Sherman, Hancock, and all of our noted Indian fighters. For cool judgment and thorough knowledge of all that pertains to military affairs, none of them, in my opinion, can be said to excel General Nelson A. Miles.

"Ah, what a man he is! I know. We have been shoulder to shoulder in many a hard march. We have been together when men find out what their comrades really are. He is a man, every inch of him, and the best general I ever served under."

"Conqueror and conciliator of Indian tribes," reads the inscription on Miles's memorial tablet in the Washington Cathedral. It is a fitting epitaph.

BIBLIOGRAPHY

Burton, Theodore Elijah, *John Sherman, American Statesman.* Boston: Houghton Mifflin Co., 1906.

Clum, Woodworth, *Apache Agent.* Boston: Houghton Mifflin Co., 1936.

Cody, Louisa Frederici, his wife, in collaboration with Courtney Ryley Cooper, *Memories of Buffalo Bill.* New York: Appleton & Co., 1919.

Cody, William Frederick, *An Autobiography of Buffalo Bill.* New York: Cosmopolitan Book Corp., 1920.

Cody, William Frederick, *The Adventures of Buffalo Bill.* New York: Harper & Brothers, 1904.

215

Craven, John J., *Jefferson Davis, Prison Life*. New York: G. W. Dillingham Co., 1905.

Custer, Elizabeth Bacon, *Boots and Saddles*. New York: Harper & Brothers, 1885.

————, *Following the Guidon*. New York: Harper & Brothers, 1890.

————, *Tenting on the Plains*. New York: Harper & Brothers, 1895.

Finerty, John F., *Warpath and Bivouac*. Chicago: Donohue Brothers, 1890.

Fisher, Clay, *Yellowstone Kelly*. Boston: Houghton Mifflin Co., 1896.

Freeman, Lewis R., *Down the Yellowstone*. New York: Dodd, Mead & Co., 1922.

Garst, Shannon, *Fighter of the Plains*. New York: J. Messner, Inc., 1944.

Gordon, Armistead C., *Jefferson Davis*. New York: Charles Scribner's Sons, 1918.

Howe, Mark A. DeWolfe, edited by, *Home Letters of General Sherman*. New York: Charles Scribner's Sons, 1909.

Johnson, Virginia W., *The Unregimented General, A Biography of Nelson A. Miles*. Boston: Houghton Mifflin Co., 1962.

Kerr, Winfield Scott, *John Sherman, His Life and Public Service*. Boston: Sherman, French & Co., 1908.

King, Charles, *Campaigning With Crook*. Norman: University of Oklahoma Press, 1964. (Original published in 1905.)

Lewis, Lloyd, *William Tecumseh Sherman, Fighting Prophet*. New York: Harcourt, Brace & Co., 1932.

McElroy, Robert M., *Jefferson Davis*. New York: Harper & Brothers, 1937.

Merington, Marguerite, edited by, *The Letters of General George Armstrong Custer and His Wife, Elizabeth*. New York: The Devin-Adair Co., 1950.

Miles, Nelson A., *Serving the Republic*. New York: Harper & Brothers, 1899.

Reynolds, Quentin, *Custer's Last Stand*. New York: Random House, 1951.

Russell, Donald B., *The Lives and Legends of Buffalo Bill*. Norman: University of Oklahoma Press, 1960.

Sandoz, Mari, *Crazy Horse*. New York: Alfred A. Knopf, Inc., 1942.

Schmitt, Martin, edited by, *General George Crook, His Autobiography*. Norman: University of Oklahoma Press, 1946. (New edition 1960.)

Sell, Henry Blackman, *Buffalo Bill and the Wild West*. New York: Oxford University Press, 1955.

Seymour, Flora Warren, *Story of the Red Man*. New York: Longmans, Green & Co., 1929.

Sherman, John, *John Sherman, Recollections of Forty Years in the House, Senate and Cabinet*. Chicago: Werner Co., 1895.

Sherman, William T., *Memoirs*. New York: Appleton & Co., 1875.

Strode, Hudson, *Jefferson Davis*. New York: Harcourt, Brace & Co., 1955.

Thorndike, R. S., edited by, *The Sherman Letters: Correspondence Between General and Senator Sherman, 1837 to 1891*. New York: Charles Scribner's Sons, 1894.

Wetmore, Helen Cody, *Last of the Great Scouts, The Life Story of Col. William F. Cody*. Duluth: Duluth Press Publishing Co., 1899.

Major General Sherman Miles (USA Ret.) has kindly made available to me important information concerning his father's career, particularly relating to the frontier days.

INDEX

219